TO BE OR NOT TO BE ... PAIN-FREE

THE MINDBODY SYNDROME

MARC D. SOPHER, M.D.

Foreword by John E. Sarno, M.D.

Illustrations by Richard Evans

D1293323

ISBN: 1-4107-0786-5 (e-book)
ISBN: 1-4107-0787-3 (Paperback)

Library of Congress Control Number: 2002096837

This book is printed on acid free paper.

Printed in the United States of America
Bloomington, IN

Illustrations by Richard Evans

1stBooks – rev. 02/13/03

To my father, Gilbert Sopher

Acknowledgements

I am grateful to Dr. John Sarno. He has been a teacher and a friend, generous in his time and support. Despite the many demands on his time, he took the time to review this and offer his always-sage advice. My wife, Michele, has been on board from day one, with her encouragement and critical eye as she reviewed the manuscript. My wonderful children, Max and Meredith, kept me in good spirits with their love, humor and sweet violin music.

I thank Richard Evans for his friendship and support. Always ready to lend an ear, Richard surprised me with the offer of his pen and artistry, for which I am doubly grateful. Pam Beauchamp was a great help with her friendship and outstanding transcription skills.

Cheers to Mac McGready for recommending that I write the book in the first place. Mac's thoughts have always been appreciated, but I'm holding off on his other suggestion for <u>GOT **TMS** ? **TRUST MARC SOPHER**</u> tee shirts.

And of course, I would like to thank my patients who took the time to hear me out, as I offered them knowledge, instead of pills.

Foreword

Now, at the beginning of the 21st century, everyone, both doctors and laymen, seems to know about stress and its affect on the body. The stress they have in mind has to do with the workplace, family matters, money, illness, and the like, and how these may make medical conditions worse. For example, it is well known that stress makes diabetes worse. But neither medicine nor the public seem to be aware that emotions play a causative role in almost all medical ills. In the first half of the 20th century many medical papers were published documenting the role of the emotions in illness, prompting one physician interested in the field, Franz Alexander, to write in 1950:

"Once again, the patient as a human being with worries, fears, hopes, and despairs, as an indivisible whole and not merely the bearer of organs--of a diseased liver or stomach--is becoming the legitimate object of medical interest."

But it was not to be. Interest in the "indivisible whole" never developed. Medicine instead began to focus on the chemistry and physics of the body and its illnesses and to ignore the possible role of emotions in health and disease. The result has been wonderful technological advances, but millions of Americans suffering needlessly from disorders whose roots are psychological, diagnostically beyond the ken of modern medicine. Emotionally induced pain disorders are epidemic in the United States and only a handful of physicians are aware of the nature of these disorders and are capable of diagnosing and treating them. Dr. Marc Sopher is one of those doctors. His book should be read by anyone suffering chronic pain of any kind or a variety of other common disorders, because his knowledge of the mindbody connection has allowed him to recognize and successfully treat many people with persistent symptoms, most of whom had tried multiple treatments without success. He is a diagnostician, a healer and doctor who knows that we are not merely complicated machines but an exceedingly complex animal whose personalities and feelings are intimately involved with everything that happens in the body.

John E. Sarno, M.D.

"Knowledge is power."

Francis Bacon

(1561-1626)

TABLE OF CONTENTS

Chapter 1

GETTING STARTED

You are probably in pain right now. That is why you are holding this book in your hands, looking for some relief. Perhaps you picked this up because you have heard of Dr. Sarno and TMS (tension myositis syndrome). Maybe a friend recommended this to you or you simply discovered it in the process of searching for answers. Your pain may be in your neck, back, legs, feet, head – it could be anywhere. With the information in this book, I am optimistic that you will be able to eliminate your pain, no matter where it is. You will do this with **knowledge.** Simply by changing how you think about the connection between your brain and body, you will begin to feel better. *I will not be* recommending oral medication, special exercises, surgery, injections, physical therapy, chiropractic manipulation, acupuncture, massage therapy, prolotherapy, or any other of the multitude of alternative therapies that have sprung up in an effort to

1

combat the explosion of chronic and recurrent pain in our society. Just knowledge.

"THERE'S NOTHING UP MY SLEEVE"

Through the process of education, you will gain a better understanding of how **psychology can affect physiology** – how your brain can be responsible for the creation of very **real** physical pain.

Armed with that knowledge, you will do battle with your brain and *stop the pain.* And you will have Dr. John Sarno to thank.

Chapter 2

WHAT IS TMS?

Much of the chronic and recurrent pain and discomfort that we all experience is psychologically induced. This is the premise of Dr. John Sarno, who coined the term "tension myositis syndrome," or TMS, to better describe and treat this pain. He gave it this name because, in the early days of his work, it was his impression that muscle (myo) was the only tissue involved. Having realized in recent years that nerves, tendons and other body systems could be targeted by the brain in the disorder that he has described, we have decided that another term would be a more accurate designation for the entire process. After much thought and discussion, he and I have agreed that the term, *The Mindbody Syndrome,* would be a better choice and would be used henceforth in place of tension myositis syndrome. This has the virtue of retaining the acronym, *TMS*, which has become familiar to many that have read Dr. Sarno's work. Dr. Sarno, an attending physician at the Howard A. Rusk Institute of Rehabilitation Medicine and professor of clinical rehabilitation medicine at the New York University School of Medicine, has helped thousands of people in his own practice and thousands more with his books explaining TMS. TMS most commonly affects the back, neck, and legs, but can affect any part of the body or organ system. Some common TMS disorders include headaches, irritable bowel syndrome, dyspepsia, gastroesophageal reflux disorder (GERD), carpal tunnel syndrome (CTS), plantar fasciitis, temporomandibular joint syndrome (TMJ), and fibromyalgia. Using today's popular lingo, TMS is a **mindbody disorder** – the symptoms arise from the mind and are experienced by the body. Thus, *The Mindbody Syndrome* is an appropriate title.

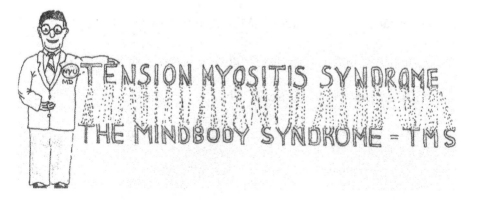

TMS is a strategy of the brain's to keep unpleasant thoughts and emotions from rising from the unconscious into the conscious mind.

The brain, through established physiologic pathways, creates pain as a distraction. By focusing our attention on physical symptoms, we keep these painful thoughts and emotions repressed. This is a very effective strategy as there is an absolute epidemic of mindbody disorders in our society.

Eliminating the pain is startlingly simple. We can banish the pain and thwart the brain's strategy by simply understanding and accepting that the pain has a psychological causation, that it is not physically based.

While much of the pain we experience has a psychological basis, it is essential to first be evaluated by your physician to determine that there is not a significant disease process. Unfortunately, if your physician does not consider TMS in the process of generating a differential diagnosis of your symptoms, it is possible that he or she will give an incorrect diagnosis. This occurs all too frequently as a physical cause is mistakenly offered. This results in a treatment plan that is often unsuccessful. As an example, many people with back pain are told that their symptoms are due to a herniated disc or disc degeneration, when in fact these findings are often incidental and normal. This helps to explain why physical therapy, medications and surgery are often unsuccessful.

Life is inherently stressful. We all have stress. We all experience some physical manifestation of it at some time. I would argue that we all have, or have had, physical symptoms with a psychological cause – TMS.

While Dr. Sarno's practice has focused more on neck, back, and limb pain, I have had the opportunity as a family physician to help many with symptoms encompassing the entire spectrum of TMS. A traditionally trained physician, I have been using Dr. Sarno's approach with great success since reading **Healing Back Pain**, his second book, and eliminating low back pain that had plagued me for nearly two years and intermittent sciatica of more than fifteen years' duration. Intrigued that reading a book could cause years of discomfort to vanish, I contacted Dr. Sarno who graciously invited me to The Rusk Institute of Rehabilitation Medicine at the New York University Medical Center to train with him.

Prompted by requests from patients with TMS symptoms mentioned but not broadly covered in Dr. Sarno's books, I offer this book based on my work with a wide variety of these mindbody disorders. As a family physician, I take care of patients of all ages, from newborns to the very old. Family doctors provide comprehensive care of their patients—they treat the *whole person*. I am responsible for not only evaluating and treating signs and symptoms of illness and disease, but also helping to keep my patients well. So, in a nutshell, I help my patients of all ages to get well when they are ailing and to stay well. Like most family doctors, I am usually the first person my patients seek out to evaluate their symptoms and examine them. This makes my experience in treating **TMS** all the more valuable to you, the reader. Able to recognize that TMS is the culprit in so many situations, I have often been able to spare many of my patients unnecessary treatment, treatment that would be unsuccessful and only prolong their period of discomfort. By more quickly directing them to the proper diagnosis, they are able to eliminate their symptoms that much more expeditiously and improve their quality of life. Isn't improved quality of life what we are all interested in, ultimately?

Being responsible for the ***whole person***, my daily encounters with patients encompass the broad spectrum of mindbody disorders. This primary care perspective can be quite challenging and even daunting at times. While there are many people who seek me out based on my reputation for TMS treatment, most others come in unsuspecting. The unsuspecting ones need to be introduced to these new, non-traditional concepts—depending on their general level of open-mindedness, this may or may not go over well. This is contrast to those that Dr. Sarno sees; his patients are already familiar with these tenets and *seek him out*. I believe this is why this book will make a good companion to Dr. Sarno's books. Because it is from my primary care perspective, it looks at a wider variety of psychologically caused disorders and may be pertinent to more people. It is also my hope that it interests more physicians, particularly family physicians, internists and pediatricians, who are on the front lines, so to speak.

This book is not meant to take the place of a comprehensive examination by a qualified physician. Not all pain is due to TMS. However, I do believe that the majority of chronic and recurrent pain does not have a structural-physical basis, but a psychological-physical one. Read on.

Chapter 3

THE PHYSIOLOGY OF TMS

Most people are quick to accept the notion that stress can cause a headache. Not a day goes by in my office without a patient acknowledging that his headache was precipitated by a bad day at work, an argument with his spouse, or a financial concern. So why couldn't stress cause pain elsewhere? Why not in the neck or back? Why couldn't it cause elbow, wrist, knee, or foot pain? We all remember those abdominal symptoms, known as "butterflies," before an important test or event. Remember, too, having "the runs" when nervous before final exams or the championship game? Imaginary? I think not. These are all examples of very real physical symptoms created by our emotions.

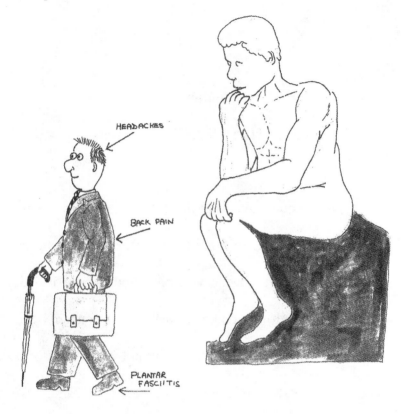

It is well understood that emotions and stress have far-reaching effects on all of the body's systems. Neurochemicals, known as neurotransmitters and neuropeptides, circulate through the entire body, affecting all areas of functioning. Some will raise the heart rate and blood pressure; others do the opposite. Some substances will cause blood vessels to constrict, restricting the blood flow and hence, the delivery of oxygen; others cause vasodilation, resulting in increased blood flow and oxygen delivery. We know that when brain serotonin levels are low, people feel depressed and despondent.

When serotonin levels are increased, mood improves and there is a sense of well-being. Stress, and our emotional response to it, will affect levels of these circulating neurochemicals.

Some basic principles of human physiology are essential to understanding where the real physical pain of TMS comes from. All of our cells require oxygen to survive and thrive. We are therefore aerobic. In the absence of oxygen, our cells die (and so do we). Blood cells circulate through the body, ferrying oxygen to cells. If there is a reduction in blood flow, oxygen delivery likewise decreases, known as hypoxemia. Relative hypoxemia causes pain, due to its effect on tissues. If the hypoxemia is great enough, tissue damage can occur. The best example of significant hypoxemia is a heart attack. In this case, one of the coronary arteries (which supplies blood and oxygen to heart muscle) becomes blocked, cutting off oxygen delivery to an area of the heart. If this obstruction is not cleared by clot-busting drugs or angioplasty (inflation of a balloon-tipped catheter in the vessel to open it), damage to an area of heart muscle occurs.

TMS pain is due to relative hypoxemia – enough reduction in blood flow to cause pain but not damage. In his books, Dr. Sarno cites elegant studies that demonstrate this. This also makes inherent sense; the typical person with TMS looks normal! The muscles in the area of their symptoms are not typically atrophying or withering away. The only caveat I would add is that the rare TMS sufferer will experience muscle atrophy from disuse due to the pain.

To summarize, our emotional state affects levels of neurochemicals that can alter blood flow to tissues, resulting in distressful symptoms. When muscles are involved, there may be pain and spasm. Tendons mildly deprived of oxygen will be painful, resulting in symptoms often diagnosed as tendonitis. Affected nerves can result in pain that has been described as burning, shooting, or sharp. Sometimes nerve involvement will cause numbness, tingling, and other disturbances of sensation described as tightness, fuzziness, etc. and occasionally even weakness of muscles in the leg or arm.

Ongoing research indicates that some neurochemicals may be solely responsible for the pain, independent of the alteration of blood flow. Ultimately understanding the exact mechanisms will be fascinating. More important though is understanding that emotions cause real physical change in the body that is then the cause of real physical symptoms. TMS is a handy acronym for these brain induced symptoms. I tell my patients that the name doesn't matter, much as "a rose by any other name would smell as sweet."

So, no matter what the exact mechanism occurring at the cellular level, the emotional state is responsible for the creation of very real physical pain. This can be stated with confidence, based on the successful treatment of thousands by Dr. Sarno and hundreds by myself. Untold others have been helped simply by reading his books – self-education. I know this as I have received letters, phone calls, and e-mails from individuals whose lives have been immeasurably improved after learning about TMS.

Skeptical? Visit www.amazon.com and look at reader comments for Dr. Sarno's books. Virtually all are enthusiastic testimonies to these concepts.

Chapter 4

PSYCHOLOGY 101

We are sentient beings. We have the capacity for thought and emotions. This is what makes us capable of the most extraordinary achievements – works of art, scientific discoveries, literature, technology, etc. It is also our downfall. Thinking and feeling allow us to experience both positive and negative emotions. We all seek joy and happiness, but reality intercedes and we all experience sadness and disappointment, anger and frustration. The ability to comprehend the concept of future offers us all the charming sensation of worrying.

As I said earlier, life is stressful. Even if we are happy and feel good about our families, jobs and finances, we all experience stress. Stress, anger, conflict arise from three main sources. There are everyday issues such as: our home and work responsibilities, worrying about our children, worrying about our parents, the inconsiderate drivers, the long line at the market, etc. Some of us have experienced much emotional distress in childhood. Even if we have made peace with it, it is still there, a potential source of unpleasant feelings. Our personalities also predispose us to these emotions. If we have high expectations for ourselves, if we are ambitious and place great demands on ourselves, if we are very conscientious about our performance, then these perfectionist traits are causes of stress. If we go out of our way to help and care for others, even to the point of self-sacrifice, then these "goodist" traits also create stress as we make our needs subordinate to those around us.

These personality traits are not undesirable—they make us successful, kind and considerate. But it is essential to understand how these very qualities can contribute to the accumulation of stress, anger and conflict. The way our brains work, we repress unpleasant thoughts and emotions. They find a home in the unconscious. This is a very good defense mechanism—it allows us to move on and take care of our responsibilities and be nice people that others like and respect. Unfortunately, we can only hold so much of these unpleasant thoughts and emotions in the unconscious. Accumulated anger, stress and conflict become RAGE. This RAGE wants to rise to consciousness, but we usually do not let this happen. If it were to happen, we might rant and rave and do things which would not be acceptable--things that would make others not think well of us. To distract us from these unpleasant thoughts and emotions, our brain creates pain, real physical pain. In our society it is acceptable, even "in vogue", to have certain symptoms, like back pain, headaches and reflux. When we focus on our pain, we are distracted from these causes of RAGE. This is a brilliant strategy on the part of the brain. Why does this occur? No one can know for sure, but we know this happens because by learning about it, we can stop it. We can stop it and thereby eliminate the pain.

Before we go any further, it is necessary to review some basic concepts of psychology, courtesy of Dr. Freud. Dr. Sarno summarizes these concepts very well in **The Mindbody Prescription** – I recommend it to all.

EGO, ID, AND SUPEREGO – THE TUG OF WAR

Our minds have three distinct components. The **Id** is the child within. It is that part of us which is self-centered, pleasure-seeking, irrational, and irresponsible. The **Superego** is the parent; it is our conscience. It tells us what is right and what is wrong. It makes us responsible and rational. While the Id will seek immediate gratification, the Superego, in seeking to do what is right, will delay or even avoid gratification. The **Ego** is the adult, caught between the Id and Superego. It is the mediator, balancing the pull between pleasure and irresponsibility on one hand, and responsibility and "doing the right thing" on the other hand. It is a constant tug-of-war. This internal conflict is within us all and is a continual source of stress. Do not forget that. Independent of other sources of stress, there is that ongoing conflict, **IN ALL OF US**.

Dr. Sarno has explained how the Superego has responsible, perfectionist, and "goodist" traits. Having perfectionist qualities means that we put additional pressure on ourselves to do certain tasks well, to succeed at challenges and to be well thought of – to have others recognize our abilities. A "goodist" does for others first, puts the welfare of others before his own – even to the point of self-sacrifice. Sound familiar? Any decent parent should recognize "goodism" in themselves. Perfectionist traits reflect back on self-esteem issues.

It is the rare individual who truly has no self-esteem issues. Virtually all of us have doubts about our own value, our worthiness. We question whether we are a good friend, spouse, or parent. Are our parents proud of us; are we a good child to them? Do we like the person that we see in the mirror?

SELF ESTEEM

These are all normal self-esteem concerns. What if parents or spouses have mistreated us? What if we've been bullied and picked on by peers? Imagine then how self-esteem would suffer and how much internal stress that would create. So many of the most severe TMS patients I've seen are children of alcoholic and abusive parents.

The Id, Ego, and Superego are the emotional components of the mind. Physiologically, referring to the brain's hardware, there are the conscious, unconscious, and subconscious components.

The conscious mind is that which we are aware of – our awake being. The subconscious mind can be thought of as the neural pathways – how our senses operate, taking in information from our environment, synthesizing it, and storing it.

RESERVOIR OF RAGE

The unconscious mind is the site of repressed and suppressed emotions. It is where the "reservoir of rage" lurks. The reservoir of rage is Dr. Sarno's term and I think it provides a compelling image for the origins of pain.

Unpleasant thoughts and emotions may be pushed into the unconscious, as they are difficult to bear. If we attempted to deal with them, it is possible that we would somehow become incapacitated in one of two ways. The Id could take over and angry, belligerent behavior would occur. In my lectures I refer to a ranting, raving lunatic, someone in need of a straitjacket. But no, behaving like that is not acceptable, so we push those thoughts away rather than act inappropriately and be ostracized (causing further reduction in self-esteem). Or, we could become paralyzed with grief, unable to function in the face of unpleasantness. But no, we don't do that either, because then we'd be shirking our responsibilities.

Some examples:

#1 Richard is getting ready to leave work on a Friday evening. Monday is a holiday and he has plans to take his family to the beach for a long holiday weekend. His boss stops by just then and asks Richard for the completed presentation on the Smith Project.

Richard expresses surprise at the request as he was told this was not due for another two weeks. His boss assures him that he emailed Richard earlier in the week with the change of plan and the report must be ready for the presentation Tuesday morning. The future success of the firm is riding on this.

So, how do you think Richard responds? Does he rant and rave at his boss, refuse to complete the task and threaten to quit? Not likely. More likely he apologizes to his family and spends the long weekend readying the presentation for Tuesday morning. This conscious act is suppression of anger and adds to the reservoir of rage.

#2 Susan's father is an alcoholic. The house is relatively quiet until he comes home late in the evening, drunk. When he is drunk he lashes out, verbally and physically, at Susan and her mother. Her grades are never good enough, the house never clean enough. His tirades are frightening and demanding and on Saturday night he was at his darkest. He struck Susan across the face, fracturing her cheek.

Her mother, trying to stop the onslaught, was also struck, and suffered multiple contusions on her chest and arms.

At school on Monday, Susan tells friends that she slipped on the icy porch stairs and reassures them she'll be fine. Susan, who could understandably withdraw as a response to her situation, soldiers on, trying to put a bright face before the world. In order to function, she has repressed the emotions that would be expected in such a horrible situation.

Repressing (unconsciously) or suppressing (consciously) thoughts and emotions that are unpleasant, disagreeable, or unacceptable allows us to continue on, but adds to the **reservoir of rage**. It helps to think of rage as accumulated stress. Not all sources of stress are equal – some may be annoying nuisances, while others may be enormous. This is a critical concept. I have seen many patients who struggle with it. If they are unable to conceive of a source of rage, or a serious stressor, they may doubt that they have this reservoir in their unconscious. Remember, the reservoir can fill with unpleasant thoughts and emotions of all sizes. Another very important concept, *reservoirs come in all sizes.*

You will see why this is important in a moment.

Dr. Sarno has identified three potential sources for this rage in the unconscious.

In each person the quantity from each source will vary.

1. Internal conflict (this is the self-imposed pressure referred to earlier – the clash of Id and Superego. It also comes from perfectionist and goodist traits).

2. Stresses and strains of daily life.

3. The residue of anger from infancy and childhood.

Now you understand about the reservoir of rage. These unpleasant thoughts and emotions "strive to rise to consciousness." That would be completely unacceptable. To prevent this from happening, ***the brain creates pain as a distraction***. As a society we are very somatically focused, preoccupied with every ache or pain. By focusing our attention on physical symptoms, we keep these painful thoughts and emotions repressed. This is a very effective strategy as there is an absolute epidemic of mindbody disorders in our society.

If you've just completed reading this section and find it to be crystal clear, turn the page and carry on. If not, re-read it. It is critical to understand that **WE ALL** have this **RESERVOIR OF RAGE**. Some people believe that if they are not depressed, not anxious, or unable to pinpoint a major source of stress or worry in their lives, then this material does not pertain to them. Too many get hung up here. I've heard people say that their childhood was fine, they are happily married, have great kids, and love their jobs – how could they have TMS? Remember, within all of us is the tug-of-war between Id and Superego. This is a huge part of the reservoir of rage. Simply add to this everyday worries – about our children, our aging parents, our own health and mortality, and there is more than enough "fuel" in the unconscious to cause the creation of distracting symptoms.

Another misconception is that the onset of pain must coincide with some obvious source of stress. While this can sometimes occur, like getting a headache on a bad day, it often is not the case! This can be a difficult obstacle for people to get over. So many times people insist that everything is *fine*, that the pain began on vacation or when everything in their life was grand, that they didn't do *anything*. They will say, "Why now?" This may cause serious doubt for them, that TMS can't be the cause. Go back to the **Reservoir of Rage**. There is always stress, even if life is good! We all worry to some degree and we all have the eternal, internal conflict between the Id and Superego. Like the straw that breaks the camel's back, some little unpleasant thought, emotion or stressor is tossed into the reservoir, which is now threatening to overflow. The brain will not allow it to overflow, or rise to consciousness—it creates pain, to distract us and keep the reservoir and its contents hidden in the unconscious. And perhaps, just perhaps, by creating pain, the brain not only causes distraction but the expansion of that reservoir.

Chapter 5

CONDITIONING

We are animals. That is not social commentary, but a biological fact. Animals can be trained or conditioned, to have a certain response to a specific stimulus or trigger. Pavlov's famous canines learned to salivate when they heard a bell. Your own pooch may become very excited each time you take out the can opener. Conditioning can be thought of as learned responses, and we become conditioned just like other species.

CONDITIONING PART 1

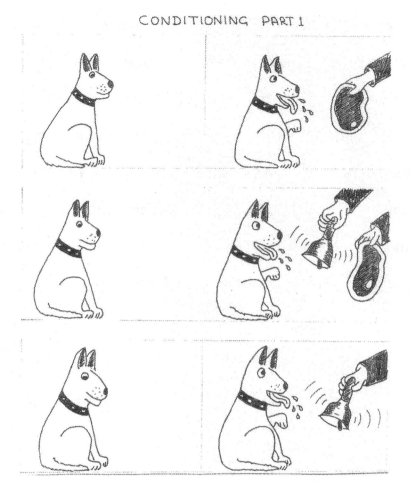

Here is an example:

You are sitting at your desk, writing a letter, and drop your pen. When you reach down to the floor to pick it up, you feel a sudden sharp pain in your low back, maybe hear a "snap" and can't straighten up. In agony, you summon your spouse who gives you ibuprofen, helps you to lay down and commiserates that your back "went out."

31

Perhaps the pain subsides over the next three to four days, but your co-workers also commiserate with you, sharing tales of similar adventures. This validates your experience and you are reinforced in your belief that bending over to pick up a pen can induce such pain. Several months later it does indeed happen again. You have been conditioned. Now you see your physician or chiropractor who confirms that improper bending, like what you did when you picked up the pen, can and will result in just these symptoms.

CONDITIONING PART 2

"I BENT OVER AND POP!—I FELT THIS SNAP IN MY BACK AND COULDN'T STAND UP! I WAS IN PAIN FOR WEEKS AFTER..."

Does this sound familiar? Does it seem just a tad ludicrous now? (More on this and other *flawed assumptions* in Chapter 8). Are we really so fragile that such a benign action could induce so much pain? IT DOES NOT MAKE SENSE! The action, bending to pick up the pen, was not the cause for the pain but a **trigger** for the creation of pain. What really occurred was that your reservoir of rage was threatening to overflow. Unpleasant thoughts and emotions, striving to rise into consciousness, had to be held back. Think of it as a pot of boiling water, needing a lid to prevent it from spilling over. To prevent the overflow, your brain seized the opportunity – the convenient presence of the trigger – to create pain, to zing you and distract you.

Back problems seem to be the most common, so I think it is no surprise that there are a multitude of "triggers" that people believe in as the cause of their pain.

Improper lifting technique

Soft mattress

Old mattress

Soft chair

Chair with insufficient back support (can you see where I'll be heading with ergonomics?)

Floor too hard

Too much time standing up (suddenly, we cannot tolerate gravity!)

And it goes on and on. Each individual can note a specific activity that can reliably cause discomfort – hey, we are all unique. I have patients tell me they can do "x" but not "x + 1" of a certain activity. Or they can do "x" but only every other day, not daily. As a result, each person constructs their own reality with various limits and rules for activities. The list of *triggers* is infinite. Some are convinced they can run, but not bike, or they get hip, knee or foot pain. Others tell me the exact opposite! Some can stand but not sit; others can sit but not stand. Laying down induces pain; others feel best when laying down—all for the same set of symptoms. Some can throw a ball but not drive a car, type or hold a newspaper without arm, elbow or hand pain. The variety of beliefs about foods and their effects on the gastrointestinal tract is astounding. THIS IS RIDICULOUS! Yet, we become conditioned and have expectations. I will counter again and again that we cannot be this fragile. If we were, we would be extinct!

If this is hitting home for you, you've probably figured out what the answer is.

Think differently, undo the conditioning, re-program your mind. For some this will come naturally and they will see results quickly. For most, this will be hard work. This is about changing habits and change rarely comes easy.

Chapter 6

NOT PLACEBO

A placebo has been defined as "a substance containing no medication and given merely to humor a patient." A placebo may also refer to a treatment modality other than medication. Almost any type of treatment (excluding an obviously toxic or harmful intervention) has a favorable response rate of approximately 30%, known as the placebo response.

The notion of a placebo response is well accepted in medicine. Why does a placebo response occur? It is indicative of the role of psychological factors in both disease and wellness. Most people do not wish to be ill or in pain. It is the rare individual who receives significant reward for their suffering. In fact, most who do receive some type of monetary compensation for their symptoms (i.e., "worker's compensation" or disability payments) would gladly give this up for relief of their discomfort. So, there is a sincere desire to be well – that is one piece of the placebo puzzle. Another significant component is the physician's (or other practitioner's) belief in the treatment offered. "Mrs. Jones, this *will* help you" has a power if delivered with conviction. Combine these two pieces with other information the patient has received – advice from well-meaning friends and family ("this helped me, so it will help you"), media coverage of health topics – and the stage is set. But alas, should a placebo response occur, it will be temporary. It must be so because it is not the correct treatment.

Most of the patients I've seen have had many types of treatment, with no response to some and only temporary response to others (placebo!). These treatments have included oral medications, injections, manipulation (chiropractic and osteopathic), physical therapy, massage, surgery, orthotic devices, etc. Of course they do not have long-term success – they have not received the appropriate treatment, which is treatment of TMS. Treatment of a psychologically caused symptom with a physical modality (pill, injection, surgery, etc.) is doomed to failure!

The success rate of Dr. Sarno's approach is 70 to 80%. SEVENTY TO EIGHTY PERCENT! This is more than double the placebo response, so it cannot be a placebo. It is also not a temporary response – it is relief that remains over time. Yes, some people will experience a return of symptoms at some point, but armed with knowledge, they will succeed at eliminating their discomfort – usually quickly. More on this later.

Chapter 7

A WORD ABOUT PHYSICIANS

So, why haven't any of the physicians you've seen mentioned TMS as a possible cause for your symptoms? You may have guessed that TMS is not currently considered by those in mainstream medicine because it is not part of their medical education. As someone who has received excellent traditional medical training, through four years of medical school and three years of residency training in family medicine, I can tell you that we are taught to find physical or structural causes for physical symptoms. Yes, we learn psychiatry and psychology, but there the focus is on mental health disorders such as depression, anxiety, schizophrenia, psychoses, and bipolar disorder. The only connection of psychological factors to physical symptoms comes with discussion of headaches, irritable bowel syndrome (sometimes), and some anxiety related symptoms (palpitations, chest tightness, throat tightness, etc.). In my experience, the most enlightened physician might go so far as to acknowledge that *stress may make any existing physical symptoms worse*, but would not suggest that there could be a psychological cause for the physical symptoms.

All of this goes back to the concept of differential diagnosis. **Differential diagnosis** is the process by which the physician obtains information from the patient (the history), does an appropriate physical examination (the physical), orders diagnostic studies (blood tests, x-rays, MRI, etc.), and then interprets this amassed data to come up with a list (long or short) of the most likely causes for the symptoms. Then, a treatment is offered based on the most likely diagnosis. This is the art of medicine – selecting the proper diagnosis so the most appropriate treatment can commence. But what if the proper diagnosis is not made? Well, sometimes people will improve, either due to the natural abilities of the body to heal or due to a placebo response. More often than not, there is a minimal response or a temporary response to the therapeutic intervention. This is what happens when physical symptoms due to TMS are treated with traditional or even alternative modalities. If the correct diagnosis is not made, how can the correct treatment be offered?

Don't get me wrong. The physicians that you have seen mean well. I truly believe that physicians choose their careers in medicine to help others. They do wish to heal, to make people well – it is a worthwhile and gratifying endeavor. So, based on their knowledge and experience, they honestly and sincerely offer treatment that they believe will help. *But their knowledge base is not complete.* That last sentence has not won me friends in the medical community, but I have no doubt about its truth. As long as physicians are not aware of the critical role of psychological factors in the causation of physical symptoms, they will be hampered in their efforts to heal.

So why are physicians so reluctant to embrace TMS theory? For starters, it is difficult to measure. The scientific approach mandates that any treatment be evaluated by formal testing, involving control groups, "blind" evaluations, "double blind" protocols, etc. Too often TMS physicians are dismissed by colleagues who state that the TMS treatment results are "anecdotal." The implication is that our results are invalid because we do not employ scientific protocol. To be blunt, this would be absolutely impossible. To treat someone with TMS, that individual must believe that their physical symptoms have a psychological basis. Period. You cannot inflict TMS treatment on someone who believes that their symptoms have a physical cause – be it a disc problem, heel spur, carpal tunnel problem, etc. It cannot be done. This has to do with the extensive conditioning that has occurred (*see Conditioning chapter*).

In addition to being difficult to measure with traditional scientific protocols, it is extremely time consuming to put into practice. It is much simpler to prescribe a pill, recommend physical therapy or surgery, than to explain to someone how his *very real* physical symptoms can have a psychological cause. If this concept is entirely new to the patient, they are likely to be very disappointed. More often than not, they were hoping for a quick fix – some physical treatment or other that would quickly alleviate their pain. Based on their conditioning and experience, this is often the expectation. Upon hearing that their symptoms likely have a psychological cause, many believe they are being told their symptoms are not real, that they are imaginary. Worse yet, they may believe they are being told that they are hypochondriacs, that they are "crazy," or that it is "all in their head." This can strain even the best doctor-patient relationship. Much time must be spent carefully explaining how psychology can and does affect physiology. So much easier to write a prescription!

Ultimately I am confident that TMS theory will be part of mainstream medicine for the simple reason that it is correct and is more successful at alleviating pain than any other modality. As more and more people are helped with this approach, physicians will have to take notice. Besides, knowing how awesome and complex the brain is, doesn't it seem rather shortsighted to discount the role that the brain can play with regard to bodily sensations?

Chapter 8

CHALLENGING ASSUMPTIONS

To accept and embrace TMS theory, it is essential to "think outside of the box." By this I mean putting aside what you've been told until now about the cause and treatment for your symptoms, **WHATEVER THEY ARE**. This is probably the most difficult part of the healing process. You must challenge assumptions that have been provided by every imaginable source – physicians, physical therapists, alternative practitioners, all forms of media, well-meaning friends, etc. These assumptions are taken at face value as truth, but they are often not only untrue, but contribute to further suffering. (In fact, Dr. Sarno recommends forgetting everything you've ever been told about the cause of your pain, what makes it better or worse, and how it should be treated.)

This is not to say that these sources mean to cause harm. They are utilizing the knowledge base that they've acquired to offer help.

When this information is proffered, it then becomes incorporated into our own knowledge base as we struggle to understand our bodies and symptoms. This is part of the conditioning process. We use the data at hand to make sense of what we experience. If these explanations are incomplete or false, we are then led down a path that will fail. When we focus our energies on an inappropriate therapeutic process, this results in the **nocebo** response – the opposite of placebo, as a useless intervention may actually cause harm. The harm is the perpetuation of symptoms through the wrong modality and misinformation. The longer we struggle, the longer the symptoms persist, the longer we are exposed to incorrect advice, the deeper the hole becomes.

In essence, we have been trained to accept and expect our symptoms.

Here are some examples of **flawed assumptions**:

1. **Healing may be prolonged for indefinite periods of time**.
   Unless someone has an unusual immune deficiency or terminal illness, he will heal promptly following an injury. Most simple bone fractures heal in four to six weeks. Dr.

Sarno likes to point out that the femur, the largest bone in the body, will heal in this time if broken. Muscle and tendon strains and ligament sprains heal within six to eight weeks, and often more quickly. So it is absurd to believe that persistent pain at the site of an injury is due to a failure to heal.

2. **<u>We are fragile</u>**.

Perhaps the single most absurd assumption put forth by the medical establishment is that the spine is inherently weak. We are told, completely erroneously, that we were meant to walk on all fours, and that by walking on two legs (bipedal) and being upright, we put excessive stress on the spine. I tell all of my patients that the spine is strong! We have evolved over millions of years to be bipedal creatures. If being bipedal made us so weak and fragile, surely we would have been wiped off the face of the earth! Imagine our ancestor, Nog, out hunting and gathering, avoiding predators: "ugh, honey, could you please hunt and gather today? My back went out while I bent over to drink at the stream." We'd be extinct if our backs weren't able to tolerate standing, let alone physical activity. With this false notion about the spine has blossomed

a multitude of absurdities.

"HONEY, WHAT DO YOU THINK
YOU ARE DOING?!? GET BACK
DOWN ON ALL 4'S THIS MINUTE!
WE'RE NOT SUPPOSED TO BE UPRIGHT!"

3.   **Never bend over at the waist; always bend at the knees**.

Again, are we so fragile that simply bending at the waist

should cause the back "to go out" and cause intense, persistent

pain? Ridiculous.

4.   **An old mattress may be the cause for back pain. A new,**

firm mattress is necessary for good back health.

With apologies to my dear friend in the mattress industry, this is silly! When we are recumbent and sleeping, the body is at rest. How could such a benign activity cause pain! If anything, sleeping arrangements have only improved over the centuries – our backs (and bodies) should be healthier. Our ancestor, Nog, had to make do without an Englander™ orthopedic model.

5. **If a chair is too soft and without adequate back support, it can cause back pain.**

This is where I refer to Monty Python and their Spanish Inquisition skit. "Oh no, not the comfy chair!" The false assumption here is that the act of sitting, being at rest, can cause pain! Virtually every patient I've seen with back pain has told me that sitting in the wrong chair will cause back pain and/or sciatica and this has been reinforced by their various practitioners. An entire industry has sprung up, creating back supports, "ergonomic chairs," etc. All nonsense.

"OH NO, NOT THE COMFY CHAIR!"

6. **Repeatedly doing an activity, which someone has been trained to do, can cause chronic pain.**

This refers to repetitive stress or motion disorders (RSD, RMD) that are currently the rage. The worker's compensation industry is burgeoning, thanks to this notion. Let me explain further. Many workers in the United States (this disorder is far less common outside of the US) do some type of repetitive activity in the workplace. Some work with a mouse pad and keyboard; others work in assembly or manufacturing. When an individual does a new activity, the newly recruited muscles may experience soreness. This may occur if someone tackles a household project, new sport, or a new work-related task. With repetition (also known as training), those muscles strengthen and become more proficient at the task. This is the conditioning response. A good example is running – this is what allows a runner to go faster and/or farther. So, the longer someone is at a task, the better they are conditioned for it; they become more efficient, it becomes easier to perform, and they become LESS SUSCEPTIBLE to injury.

Every physician knows this basic fact of human physiology, yet the myth of RSD/RMD not only persists, *it is thriving!* A prominent orthopedist stated that the only way a keyboard should cause pain would be if it fell from a great height! When presented with this concept, a patient offered this insight. Now in her 60's, she worked several decades ago in a large secretarial pool, typing all day with her colleagues on manual typewriters. She could not recall anyone ever having arm/wrist/hand pain or other symptoms typical of carpal tunnel syndrome (CTS) that is now epidemic.

7.   **Pain may be due to misalignment of the spine or pelvis.**

This is often a practitioner's claim and is total nonsense. Vertebrae are extremely stable, not susceptible to being "out of alignment" as chiropractors would have you believe. An extraordinary framework of ligaments, muscles and tendons maintain the spine's stability. It would be a catastrophic event if vertebrae were to "dislocate" – this can result from massive trauma, like a high-speed motor vehicle accident, or fall from a significant height, and could result in serious damage to the spinal cord. Fortunately, this is rare. There are other medical conditions, also uncommon, which can result in destruction of vertebrae and subsequent spinal cord trauma.

Some practitioners will point out "abnormalities" on x-ray that are rarely significant or due to a process that could result in symptoms. Sometimes these findings are simply due to posture, muscle tightness or spasm; other times there are congenital conditions, variations from normal, that are likely present since birth and not a cause for symptoms. In their effort to pinpoint a physical cause for very real physical symptoms, they can then justify the application of their physical "remedy."

8.   **If a test result is abnormal, it must be the cause of physical symptoms.**

With the availability of CT and now MRI scanners, it is possible to obtain remarkable images of the body. That is the good news. The bad news is that many of these images will be reported as abnormal – one study reported in the New England Journal of Medicine that greater than 60% of spine MRIs showed abnormalities, the same percentage in those without pain as with pain. Virtually every person over 20 who has a spine MRI will be told they have degenerative disc disease, disc herniation, degenerative changes, or some other abnormality. As these findings are present equally, no matter whether symptoms exist, it is Dr. Sarno's and my contention that these are incidental, rarely the cause for pain. Unfortunately, physicians are taught to find a physical cause for physical symptoms and thus tell their patients about their "back problem."

Being told that you have a "problem" or "condition" can aid the "nocebo response." This is the opposite of the placebo response. With a placebo, belief in a worthless remedy can provide relief, almost always temporary, due to the desire to be well and faith in the value of the remedy. With a nocebo, symptoms will persist or intensify as a result of being informed, incorrectly, that a significant defect or problem is to blame. This is a critical part of conditioning – coming to believe that certain actions, circumstances, or aspects of the environment are the cause of symptoms, when in fact the cause lies in the mind. More on conditioning in chapter 5.

Chapter 9

FIXING YOUR _____ (FILL IN THE BLANK)

Thousands of people have reached me through the Internet, seeking relief. Virtually all have read one of Dr. Sarno's books and are attempting to put his approach into practice. A common theme is they believe that TMS is the cause of their symptoms, but that Dr. Sarno didn't go into depth discussing their particular problem. This was a large part of what motivated me to write this book. So, search for your body part or organ system and read on.

Chapter 10

HEADACHES

When I first introduce an unsuspecting patient to TMS concepts, I usually start by discussing headaches. I do this for two simple reasons: 1) *everyone* has had headaches, and 2) *everyone* believes that headaches may be related to stress or psychological factors. Even physicians believe that most headaches are somehow caused by stress or worry! No one would deny that the pain of a headache was not real; in fact, some migraines can be incapacitating. So, headaches are excellent examples of physical pain that is very real, created by the brain to distract us from thinking about unpleasant thoughts and emotions. Remember, always check with your regular doctor to rule out something serious.

There are other important factors to take into consideration. Many with chronic or recurrent headaches take a lot of pain medication to alleviate their discomfort. This is a two-edged sword; while analgesics can provide pain-relief, regular use can result in rebound headaches (in the case of discontinuation of NSAIDs, such as aspirin, ibuprofen or acetaminophen) or withdrawal headaches (from discontinuation of narcotics, like codeine, Percocet, Vicodin, etc.). Others ingest large quantities of caffeine, or caffeine-containing medication, that temporarily reduce headache, but can result in withdrawal headaches as a result of discontinuation or dramatic reduction in intake. These situations are excellent examples of what may happen when a physical modality (in this case a medication) is used to treat a psychological problem.

How to get rid of headaches? Use the same approach outlined in Chapter 30. Once you succeed at stopping the headache, use this success to keep the headaches from returning. Spending even a small amount of time each day reflecting on TMS principles works as **preventive medicine**. You do not need to allow your brain to create this pain, this distraction.

Chapter 11

WHIPLASH - A PAIN IN THE NECK, PART I

Most people believe that chronic pain from a "whiplash" injury is a common and expected outcome following a hit-from-behind motor vehicle accident. Chronic whiplash refers to neck pain that extends well beyond the time of the accident. In addition to neck pain, some also experience chronic headaches, back pain and a variety of other symptoms.

Whiplash is nonsense. These people have musculoskeletal TMS triggered by the rear-end collision.

Well done comparative studies show that in cultures without "preconceived notion of chronic pain arising from rear end collisions, and thus no fear of long term disability, and usually no involvement of the therapeutic community, insurance companies, or litigation, symptoms after an acute whiplash injury are self limiting, brief, and do not seem to evolve to the so-called late whiplash syndrome."

SOMEWHERE IN LITHUANIA.....   "YOU'LL BE FINE SOON"

SEVERAL WEEKS LATER....
"HOW'S YOUR NECK?"
"PERFECT! IT HEALED IN NO TIME."

When cultures have a system that provides medical care for mindbody disorders, including compensation for disability, those disorders tend to spread in epidemic fashion. This is not because the patients are faking or would rather not go back to work, but because the condition has been diagnosed as "physical" and medical insurance will pay for treatment. It has been demonstrated, specifically regarding whiplash, that if medical insurance is not available, the epidemic does not develop.

Furthermore, when cultures that have a system reinforcing the notion of chronic pain following a rear-end collision make legislative changes in their tort compensation laws, there is a decreased incidence and improved prognosis of whiplash injury. Put more simply, **elimination of compensation for pain and suffering eliminates pain and suffering.**

Let's backtrack now. You are the belted driver of a vehicle sitting at a stoplight when suddenly you are struck from behind by another vehicle. Somehow, the driver of that vehicle, perhaps engrossed in a cell phone conversation, doesn't notice the red light or the presence of your car at a stop, in his path. CRASH! Fortunately you do have your seatbelt on, but the force of the collision snaps your head backward (a body at rest tends to remain at rest) and then forward. Depending on the force of the impact, the neck muscles may be totally unaffected or there may be some strain. The headrests now built into modern cars diminish the possibility of significant muscle strain or more severe injury.

What happens next exemplifies the sad history of mindbody disorders that are not recognized for what they are. The brain uses the physical incident as a trigger and initiates the process of TMS. Hours, days or even weeks later, the person begins to experience pain in the neck or shoulders or upper back, sometimes in the low back, and occasionally in one or both arms. The symptoms are attributed to the whiplash incident and the epidemic is on its way. The availability of medical care merely facilitates the epidemic spread of the disorder, but it is the fact that it is in vogue and has been misdiagnosed by doctors, that more and more people will tend to get it. Given that our bodies have a wondrous capacity to heal following trauma, what should happen is that after a brief period of discomfort your body heals and the pain leaves – four weeks' maximum. This is absolutely the norm in countries where there are no legal, social, or medical supports for chronic pain following whiplash injury.

But *if* you believe that chronic pain may follow such an injury, *if* you have friends, family, or coworkers that have chronic pain following such an event, *if* you know of someone who collected a substantial sum of money for "pain and suffering" as a result of such an accident, *if* you are enticed by the advertisements of the personal injury lawyers that literally scream at you from every type of media, *then* your pain may persist beyond the expected time of healing. Why? Because of conditioning.

Sadly, the medical system feeds into this. If your physician tells you that chronic whiplash does occur, this may have a **nocebo** effect – more fuel for errant conditioning. If you are referred for physical treatments, like physical therapy, massage, acupuncture, or chiropractic, you are being told that you have a physical problem that might be remedied in this fashion. Pain medications and muscle relaxants may offer relief, but only temporarily. This perpetuates the notion of a physical cause.

It is inevitable that x-rays, CT scans, or MRIs will be done and will reveal abnormalities. There is nothing quite so powerful for conditioning as showing someone a picture highlighting the "culprit" – degenerative changes, disc disease, WHATEVER. This is despite the fact that abnormalities on these studies occur with the same frequency in those with pain as those *without* pain. Now you're a goner.

The pain is real. Don't for a minute think that it is not.

Your brain has used the acute whiplash injury as a **trigger**. What a perfect spot to put pain – pain that has a psychological cause, not a physical one. Remember, **IT IS A DISTRACTION**, keeping those unpleasant thoughts and emotions from surfacing from the unconscious.

Chapter 12

HANDS UP!

Right behind headaches, back pain and foot pain is hand and wrist pain, often diagnosed as carpal tunnel syndrome, or CTS. Symptoms may include pain (burning, aching, stabbing, etc.), numbness, tingling, and/or weakness from the forearm to the fingers. Sometimes constant, sometimes intermittent, triggers may include repetitive activity (like keyboard or mouse work) and even sleep! Fortunately, recent studies may help to dispel these myths. Remember, a keyboard can only cause discomfort if it falls from a great height!

CTS is often discussed as a repetitive stress disorder (RSD) or injury (RSI). The patients I've seen with CTS complaints are often doing repetitive tasks, in assembly or at a factory machine. Think of them as athletes who have trained at an activity or task and it becomes apparent that their symptoms can't be caused by their work. Even if they are obese smokers who cannot climb a flight of stairs without huffing and puffing, they are uniquely prepared for their work by virtue of that repetition. With training, with repetition we become more capable, not less so. **We aren't so fragile, remember?** Truth be told, many of the tasks that these people perform are not physically demanding, they are just done over and over again.

So, why the explosion of CTS? Well, the powers that be have declared that RSI is a physical problem with a physical cause (repetitive activity, improper ergonomics, etc.). It has been made a legitimate and acceptable cause of pain (think "in vogue"). The trigger is in place, the system recognizes it, and – voila – a mindbody disorder may flourish.

Current CTS treatment includes anti-inflammatory drugs, steroid injections, wrist splints, physical therapy, occupational therapy, and if all else fails, surgery. I've seen many treatment failures. By this I mean no response or temporary relief only. Why? Because a physical modality cannot cure a problem with a psychological cause.

Let's go back to these patients with CTS. Susan does data entry at her computer for eight hours each day. She does not love her job; she finds it boring and the pay is barely enough to make ends meet. She works full-time and feels guilty that her kids have to go to daycare after school. Bob works assembling circuit boards. He often works overtime – the extra income allows his wife to work only part-time so she can spend more time with their children. Bob feels his supervisor doesn't appreciate him. Bob's father just learned he has lung cancer. Susan and Bob also have the same internal conflicts that we all do. Now do you know why they hurt? Their pain is from TMS and they got better when they recognized this.

Scott is a pilot, married with two children, who came to see me for evaluation of wrist and thumb pain plaguing him for more than one year. He was certain it was arthritis or possibly carpal tunnel syndrome. While taking his full history, he also complained of chronic neck and back pain and recurrent testicular discomfort, the last diagnosed as epididymitis.

Conscientious, thoughtful and caring, he saw that his personality and the stresses of every day living could be sufficient to cause his symptoms. It is now three years of feeling well and he is able to quickly rid himself of symptoms when they recur.

Further support for how CTS is actually another manifestation of TMS comes from a recent medical paper that suggested that the cause of the malfunction of the median nerve at the wrist is a mild reduction of blood flow to the area. Hence, mild oxygen deprivation results in TMS symptoms in the hand or wrist, just as it causes TMS symptoms elsewhere in the body.

Chapter 13

BACK PAIN

Given that back pain is one of the most common of the mindbody disorders, it merits a chapter. However, what I offer will only serve to summarize what Dr. Sarno has described so elegantly in **Mind Over Back Pain, Healing Back Pain**, and **The Mindbody Prescription**. So, for a more in-depth discussion of back pain, be sure to read his work.

Over more than thirty years at The Rusk Institute of Rehabilitation Medicine at the New York University Medical Center, Dr. Sarno has treated more than 10,000 patients with back pain. Approximately 80% of those patients have experienced total or significant resolution of their symptoms. This is particularly remarkable when considering the vast array of treatment modalities these patients have tried, unsuccessfully. When I saw patients with Dr. Sarno, I was struck by how "difficult" this group was. As physicians we often describe patients as "difficult" when they continue to experience unpleasant symptoms despite the best efforts of other physicians and practitioners. I do not mean "difficult" in the sense that they themselves are unpleasant or not courteous. Often these patients have been waved on their way by frustrated physicians who have not provided them with relief and have told them to "live with their pain." Can you imagine being told that you should expect to have pain forever and that you have to put up with it?

Further compounding this problem is the veritable explosion of pain clinics around the US. These pain clinics are staffed by "pain specialists" who are often anesthesiologists. I have read numerous articles and heard numerous lectures by these pain specialists in which they clearly state they cannot cure anyone, but can offer temporary pain relief. They, too, tell patients to learn to live with their pain. So they inject and prescribe medications and further the conditioning process. While many of them will acknowledge how stress can make symptoms worse, they *always* provide an explanation that delineates a *physical cause* for the physical symptoms. More conditioning that must be undone if healing is to ever occur.

So these difficult patients arrive. Months and years of back pain despite medication, injections, surgery, manipulation, acupuncture, physical therapy, etc. When these fail many turn to a host of alternative therapies. New mattresses and special chairs, back pillows and lumbar supports, neoprene corsets and magnets have been purchased, all to no avail.

Not many have stopped to think, why now? Why this epidemic of back pain? Have we, as a species, suddenly become so fragile? If we are so susceptible to injury, how is it that we have not become extinct?

I believe the exponential rise in the incidence of back pain correlates perfectly with two major societal trends in the latter half of the twentieth century. The first is the post-WWII baby boom with its attendant cultural shift towards increasing materialism and acquisition. The second is the technology revolution, a direct byproduct of which is better medical imaging. Not only do we experience more complexity and stress in our day-to-day activities, but we are bombarded by global images of conflict, destruction, and death by the ever-expanding reach of modern media.

Increasing awareness of external conflicts, coupled with the stress of daily life and our own internal conflicts makes a perfect crucible for the creation of pain. The spectacular new imaging techniques give us a seemingly magical look inside our bodies, identifying "abnormalities" that could not have been discovered before.

As I've already noted, most of these findings are very common and incidental, not the cause of symptoms. Many well-done studies bear this out. The presence of herniated or degenerative discs, degenerative joint findings, spurs and foraminal narrowing do not correlate reliably with symptoms. This goes a long way to explain why traditional physical treatment modalities fail or provide only temporary relief.

The most common complaint is discomfort in the low back or lumbar area. Sometimes it is on one side only, sometimes on both sides, and sometimes it moves around. It is often intermittent. Sometimes it radiates, causing discomfort into the groin, hip, thigh, or lower leg. Sometimes it is triggered by a certain activity or movement, other times it comes on without provocation, such as when sitting or laying down.

Because the pain is so rarely constant, I will ask patients why, if there is a physical cause (static, by definition), should the pain be intermittent? I mean, if there is a herniated disc or some other process, why should the pain come and go? How does that make sense? Also, even those who complain of "constant" pain, the reality is that there is always waxing and waning of symptoms. This is often where the idea of a "pinched nerve" or "nerve compression" comes up. As it has been well established that a neural foramen would need to be almost completely obliterated for nerve compression to occur, I think it highly unlikely that a nerve could be compressed in the periphery. "Compression" or "pinching" of a nerve implies a significant force could be continually applied to a nerve. As nerve substance is relatively soft and our tissue (fat, muscle, tendon, and ligament) is not rigid, surely there is sufficient physical space to allow nerves to transit without injury. Another fact must also be mentioned here. *Should* a nerve be continuously compressed it will not result in pain but numbness, absence of sensation!

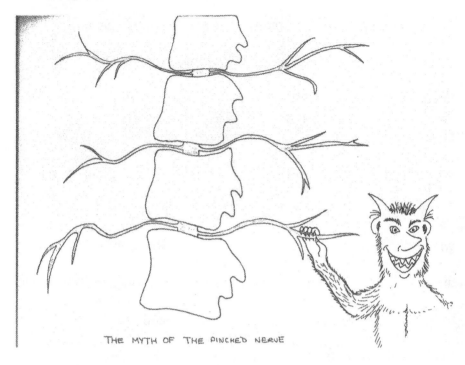

THE MYTH OF THE PINCHED NERVE

Now, I would venture to guess that any physician who took a moment to consider that last sentence would agree with it. However, most do not stop to think about it. To concur with that statement would fly in the face of our current medical education that insists on physical explanations for physical symptoms. So, the **myth of the pinched nerve** is dutifully repeated. Oh, it has its variations, such as the **myth of nerve impingement** or the dreaded, dark tunnel syndrome (carpal for forearm, wrist and hand symptoms; tarsal, a relative newcomer, for ankle and foot symptoms).

One more comment on the myth of nerve compression bears mention. The alleged compression of a single spinal nerve by a herniated disc could never produce the widespread, severe pain that is characteristic of a typical "back attack." Only a brain-induced disorder could do that by involving multiple muscles and nerves.

But, back to backs. Throughout this book I have made comments regarding back pain. The bottom line is that the overwhelming majority of back pain does not have a physical cause. Remember, we all feel a little sore after shoveling snow, moving furniture or doing a lot of yard work. That soreness is almost pleasant, a subtle reminder of the worthy activity and the satisfaction from completing a task – and it resolves within a few, short days. That nagging, ongoing back pain that occupies many of your waking moments is not due to discs, arthritis, misalignment or other physical processes. That is why there are so many people who have ongoing symptoms despite surgery, manipulation, injections, medication, etc. Sure, there might be some temporary relief, but not long term, meaningful improvement. The pain recurs and continues to distract us from those suppressed and repressed unpleasant thoughts and emotions. We think about the pain:

"What did I do this time?"

"Oh, I should not have done <u>that</u>!"

"When is the pain going to leave?"

"How am I ever going to _____, if this pain doesn't leave?"

And we despair. And we take pills. And we seek out other remedies. And we are distracted. Again, if we are so fragile that routine activities of life could induce such discomfort, how is it that our species is not extinct? **We are not so fragile!!** We have evolved to be able to handle gravity, walk upright, run, carry, lift, bend, sit, recline, stand, and just about any other activity, except fly.

Ron, now 27, remembers low back pain since age 12. His pain had worsened over the past five years, dating back to when he proposed to his wife. He described pain that was "dull, constant, burning" and could be increased by bending, sitting or standing. At times pain would travel down his leg. When an orthopedist diagnosed him with degenerative disc disease based on his MRI, he sought another opinion. The second orthopedist also did x-rays, bone scan, electromyographic studies (EMG) and blood work and confirmed the first diagnosis. NSAIDs, epidural steroid injections, physical therapy, acupuncture and chiropractic were tried unsuccessfully.

He told me, "I can't do the things I love." Ron acknowledged his perfectionism and even quit his job because he thought the work stress was contributing to his pain.

One month later he reported being much better.

Charlene Penz was 56 years old when we met. Plagued by low back pain and sciatica for more than 30 years, her pain could be intense and had worsened over the past 10 years. CT scan and MRI were read as showing extensive arthritis and degenerative disc disease and she was advised to have a multilevel fusion of her lumbar spine. The roll call of treatment prescribed by her family physician, orthopedist and neurosurgeon included NSAIDs, muscle relaxants, narcotics, oral steroids, epidural steroid injections, special exercises, physical therapy and chiropractic.

Suffering from anxiety and depression brought on by her suffering, she also took Prozac and went for counseling to try to cope better with life. "I like to do for others" was how she described herself. She had recently helped her daughter as she battled breast

cancer. Her alcoholic father had abandoned her family when she was

young.

She left her session with me, discarded her lumbar roll and drove

700 miles home. She was fine and remains so. Below is her letter:

Dear Dr. Sopher,

I wrote a letter to you last November, after my visit in October, to let

you know how well the program was working for me. I also sent a

picture along of the two of us. I was fearful of Springtime. It was

what I called the "acid test." If I could get through Spring without an

incident, I was pretty confident the rest of the Summer would be fine.

Well, I did it !!!! I'm so proud of myself. Without your support and

knowledge of the underlying problem I know my life would have

continued on in fear and pain. It's almost scary to feel this good. I

have to admit I still find myself waiting for the other shoe to drop.

When I pick up my sweet grandson (6 mo and 22 lb. and always

wriggling in my arms) I find that I don't even think about my back. I

actually pick up anything all of the time and don't think about my back. If I do have an occasional day or two of stiffness and low pain (2), I play the tape of the meeting, and hearing your voice, and listening over and over again to your words of wisdom, will usually relieve any discomfort I'm experiencing at the time. Applying all the messages which you recommended about the ID and the oxygen deprivation helps tremendously. Also, my doctor is applying the same technique when his back starts bothering him, and he is also sharing the book The Mindbody Prescription with his patients.

Thank you again Dr. Sopher. My life has done a 180 thanks to you. If you ever need a testimony from a 58-year-old woman with a history of 30 years of suffering, feel free to call. I'd make a trip up there anytime.

Sincerely,

Charlene Penz

Sally is a 30-year-old married woman with back pain for four years. Her entire back can hurt, spreading into the shoulders and down into her legs. Sitting and standing are both pain-inducing and she stopped working due to her discomfort. She has also put off starting her family. She was told that she had spina bifida occulta on

MRI and was put on a variety of medications, including Ultram, with

no relief. Physical therapy, chiropractic manipulation, acupuncture,

epidural steroid injections all were tried unsuccessfully. Sally even

went to a special pain clinic – no change.

A self-described perfectionist and goodist, she had dramatic

improvement within one month of seeing me and remains well,

several years later.

Ken is a 48-year-old gentleman with low back pain that could

radiate down the leg to his foot of more than 25 years duration. His

initial symptoms were treated with back surgery – lumbar

laminectomy. Never completely relieved, his pain intensified and he

was again diagnosed with a herniated disc. Another back surgery

followed, also with incomplete resolution of symptoms. In the year

before he came to see me, he had pain with sitting and all activities

that he formerly enjoyed like bicycling, in-line skating and hiking.

When working at his desk or computer he would stand, instead of sit.

He bought a special mattress, orthotics for his shoes and did special

exercises, in addition to the other usual treatment. His most recent

MRI, done to evaluate back pain radiating down the leg, was interpreted as showing scar tissue pressing on nerves.

During our session, Ken described himself as a perfectionist, over achiever and "people pleaser." Though happily married, he identified stress at home with his stepson's learning disability and his widower father living with him; his father had been very critical and emotionally abusive when Ken was younger. Within one month he was much improved and by three months was virtually pain-free and back to enjoying long distance bicycling and hiking. Two years later he continues to be fine, sending me emails chronicling his athletic exploits. Interestingly his other TMS equivalents, eczema and frequent urination, also resolved.

Connie described a life-long history of sciatica. Fifty years old and single, she had leg pain with sitting and running, an activity that she loved. She had given up running at the orthopedist's suggestion after her spine MRI revealed degenerative changes, multiple herniated discs and scoliosis – "a mess" in her words. Her history also included chronic foot pain, attributed to a Morton's neuroma, which was exacerbated by running.

Physical therapy, chiropractic manipulation, NSAIDs, narcotics, benzodiazepines and eventually surgery all failed to relieve her pain. So unbearable was her discomfort that she admitted to suicidal ideation.

Raised by alcoholic parents and alcoholic herself, she had been sober for a number of years. She had no problem with the idea of a reservoir of rage in the unconscious. Within three months she was much better, back to running and training for a marathon.

Henry is a 62-year-old gentleman with a history of low back pain with intermittent sciatica for approximately 30 years. Initially the pain was episodic, but over the years became more prevalent. X-rays, CAT scans, CT myelograms and MRIs were performed and at various times the following diagnoses were given: herniated disc, degenerative disc disease, osteoarthritis and spinal stenosis. Treatment strategies included: limitation of activities, special back exercises, physical therapy, anti-inflammatory medications, chiropractic manipulation, massage therapy, acupuncture and epidural steroid injections. Five years ago back surgery was performed for treatment of herniated disc without improvement of symptoms. The most recent recommendation was for a multilevel spinal fusion procedure.

During my evaluation Henry revealed that his back symptoms began during a difficult time in his first marriage. Exacerbations often occurred with times of increased stress in that marriage and in his second. Additionally, he has devoted extraordinary resources to his second wife in her lengthy battle with cancer. His personality is clearly that of the "goodist" – one who does for others, often to the point of self-sacrifice.

He was able to "think psychological" and accept that his pain had a psychological cause. Henry repudiated the physical – though his pain was real, it was not due to a physical problem, despite the findings of his diagnostic studies. He understood that the pain was created by the brain to distract him from unpleasant thoughts and emotions stored in the unconscious, the unconscious "rage" described by Dr. Sarno. He was able to eliminate his pain and resume activities that he had given up.

Jack is a 24-year-old single computer consultant who admitted that he was obsessed by his back pain. Six months earlier he developed acute low back pain while playing ping-pong. Pain could radiate down either leg to his feet and was worsened by sitting, standing and all athletic activity. He stopped running, skiing, playing basketball and flag football and lifting weights and was despondent. MRI revealed a herniated disc. Physical therapy, NSAIDs and epidural steroid injections did not help. He did not want surgery.

He acknowledged being a worrier, sometimes to the point of obsession. His mother committed suicide when he was eight and now he was contemplating moving away from his family to take a better job.

One month later he was fine and had resumed all of his activities.

Paul Teta is another long-term sufferer. 53 years old, Paul's symptoms began more than 20 years earlier while playing basketball. Pain could travel down his leg and he underwent back surgery for a herniated disc. His symptoms improved but returned, sometimes severe enough to make it impossible to work or do the athletic activities that he enjoyed.

Repeat MRI showed disc herniation and NSAIDs and narcotics did not ease his pain. Married with two children, Paul owns and operates an auto repair shop. He admits that he is a perfectionist, sometimes "high strung" or "uptight." Not wishing another surgery and wanting to resume his life, he came to see me. Two weeks later he was fine and several years later remains pain-free. Below is his letter:

Dr. Sopher – My name is Paul Teta. I recently (two weeks ago) had an appointment with you. I came with my brother, who you were nice enough to invite to the seminar. I just wanted to give you a quick update on my progress. The day I arrived for my initial exam I was in pain and also on a strong pain killer, and had been for weeks.

I had read Dr. Sarno's book twice. After you confirmed that I had TMS, you said to me, do not fear the pain for it was harmless and my back was normal. I think that statement saved me weeks of time. That evening we went to the seminar, which gave me even more confidence. I have not taken any medicine of any kind for back pain. Several days after I put on my roller blades and bladed about 10 miles. At that point my leg was killing me. I continued to blade for another eight miles and my back started to twist and I was losing the lumbar curve. I kept repeating to myself, "the pain is harmless and my back is normal." At about 19 miles the pain stopped and my leg turned warm. Afterwards I had a twenty mile drive home. I had no pain sitting for the first time. While driving home I started to scream out loud, "I'm sic, of this pain dictating my life!" I began to cry and did so for about 30 minutes (possibly childhood rage?).

After that I have taken out my running shoes (after 15 years) and resumed running. "NO PAIN." I feel 18 again. I also can bend over and can for the first time put on my socks without lying down. In my wildest dreams, I never expected to do this well. Twenty years of fear and pain erased so quickly. I have since purchased about 10 books and have given them to friends and customers of mine. THANK YOU DR. SOPHER AND DR. SARNO. I will send you a future letter of more details as soon as time permits

.

Stan is a 53-year-old whose low back pain began 10 years earlier while doing plumbing work. His pain would radiate down one leg and his subsequent diagnosis for back pain with sciatica was a herniated disc and degenerative disc disease at multiple levels. He saw an orthopedist, physiatrist and neurosurgeon. Epidural steroid injections, NSAIDs, acupuncture and physical therapy did not help. Desperate he went to a chiropractor that manipulated him thirty consecutive days. Sitting caused pain. He stopped running as this also aggravated his symptoms.

Describing himself as "very responsible, to a fault," he put a tremendous amount of pressure on himself. Happily married now with four children, his previous divorce had been very stressful. Work was very demanding. Recently his mother had passed away and he was trying hard to improve a relationship with his father that had been poor in the past.

One month later he was much improved and described being pain-free at four months. A couple of years later he is still well.

Chapter 14

NECK PAIN, Part 2

This will be a short chapter. Think of the neck as the northern part of the spine and the low back as the south. Same type of construction is present throughout the spine – vertebrae (bones), discs, muscles, ligaments and tendons. No surprise that neck symptoms are similar to those experienced lower in the back. Pain is often described as sharp, stabbing or tightness and may radiate down the back or to the shoulder and arm. This pain that moves is often referred to as radicular and explained as nerve impingement. Sound familiar? This mirrors the radiating low back pain, known as sciatica.

Sometimes neck pain is part of a whiplash injury (see chapter 11). Often someone describes simply turning their head and, wham!, sudden pain. How does it make sense that simply turning your head could induce such pain? Sometimes people state they awoke with the pain, that they must have "slept wrong." Slept wrong? Oh, I see, they must have missed those classes on how to sleep. But physicians reinforce this nonsense.

SLEPT WRONG

Torticollis, or spasmodic torticollis, is an uncommon condition causing neck pain and sometimes deformity. Posterior and lateral neck muscles remain in spasm. Not only is this extremely painful, but the spasm also results in muscle shortening on the affected side. The result of this is a head tilt – the individual keeps their head turned and tilted toward the affected side. No physical treatment does better than provide temporary relief. As a result, even potent muscle relaxants and botox injections have been tried, with disappointing results.

Because the neck is in fact located so close to the head and most accept that stress and psychological factors are involved with headaches, many are open to the possibility that neck pain may have similar causation. But, unfortunately, many others do not. So they seek physical treatments and receive injections, manipulation, surgery and all of the remedies employed in the battle of back pain with disappointing results.

Carla, a 46-year-old homemaker with one son, complained of neck, back, leg and foot pain for more than two years. Often the lower leg pain and foot pain could be a severe "burning" that prevented her from walking. She was evaluated by her primary care physician, orthopedist, neurologist, physiatrist and neurosurgeon. Along the way she also developed jaw pain for which she saw her dentist and then an otorhinolaryngologist (ear, nose and throat doctor – ENT). Spine MRI showed disc herniations in her neck and low back. Other tests, including blood work and nerve studies were normal. She received many diagnoses, including neuropathy, and was put on Neurontin (an anti-seizure medicine) when all other treatments failed. She had been active, enjoying bicycling, hiking, canoeing and cross-country skiing, but had to stop due to pain.

A worrier, Carla noted she was very concerned about her son's safety when he went to college. Her mother had died when she was only two years old and she was raised by her father's sisters as her father never re-married. He, too, had passed away recently and had always been difficult, even when he spent his last years in her home. Within two months of her appointment with me her symptoms had resolved.

Chapter 15

REPETITIVE STRESS INJURIES AND REPETITIVE STRESS

DISORDERS

Now that studies have concluded that computer keyboard work is not responsible for carpal tunnel syndrome (CTS), I have to believe that it is just a matter of time before other studies deflate the myths of other repetitive stress disorders (RSD).

I firmly believe that RSD is akin to whiplash. It exists only because of the legal, social, and medical sanctions in our society. Remove litigation, insurance companies, and practitioners wed to the mistaken belief in physical causes for all physical symptoms, and RSDs vanish. Worker's compensation has value when grievous harm occurs in the course of an occupation, but it is now totally out of control. Our legal system has run amuck. Law schools churn out more attorneys than we need. Needing to provide for themselves, lawyers have had to adapt and so have explored and exploited every nook and cranny of laws governing compensation. These opinions are not original. However, what I have to say next is.

If TMS theory enters the societal mainstream and is embraced by the medical community, the insurance industry and legislators, much of the chronic pain in our society will vanish.

While this may seem difficult to believe, it has occurred in other countries. As I said earlier, elimination of compensation for pain and suffering can eliminate pain and suffering. Imagine the ramifications! Employer costs are cut as insurance rates drop, employees take less sick time, and there is a decline in disability. Employees have fewer physical complaints and accordingly see improvement in mood. It can just snowball. Yes, I may be a dreamer, but I know it is within the realm of possibility. An exercise physiologist and expert witness in chronic pain cases, such as whiplash and RSD, requested anonymity when he agreed with me on this issue. Who dares to kill the golden goose?

Chapter 16

WORKERS COMPENSATION

I have touched on this already, with discussion of repetitive stress injuries, carpal tunnel syndrome and back and neck pain. It is necessary for me to make a few more points.

In theory, workers compensation is a good concept, rooted in fairness. Simply put, a worker injured on the job is eligible to be compensated if he has experienced significant harm that precludes or limits his ability to be gainfully employed. This deserves closer scrutiny, what I referred to earlier as challenging assumptions. Implicit in this concept is the belief that injury may arise in the course of normal work activities – activities that someone has been trained to do and that they have done in the past without difficulty (or pain). Also implicit is that this injury has resulted in pain or functional limitation that has not resolved and may not resolve. This is the foundation for the erroneous belief that certain injuries may not heal and thus result in chronic pain. This is ludicrous! This defies what we understand about human physiology, about our remarkable capacity to heal and recover.

Yes, there are certainly workplace accidents that may cause harm for which compensation is appropriate. But this must be serious trauma, like crush and amputation injuries, head trauma, etc.

Yet, it is commonly believed that simply standing on a hard surface while working can result in back, neck, hip, knee or foot pain. Not only can it result in pain, but it can result in chronic pain, pain that physical modalities cannot alleviate. And there will be money to be had. There are so many of these misconceptions; a few follow. Doing keyboard work can be hazardous, even though the modern computer keyboard requires the slightest press of the fingertips to operate. The angle of the keyboard must be just so, or pain will be inevitable. Someone who sits for their task must have their seat at the proper height, of the proper firmness, with the right back support or woe will befall them! This type of thinking has allowed the field of ergonomics to flourish. Again, the underlying flawed assumption is that we humans are fragile, that we cannot make adaptations or accommodations to our environment. We must alter our environment or suffer the consequences. It is such nonsense, this belief that we have reached this point after three million years of evolution only to be so inferior as to buckle under the demands of daily living.

Now, if ergonomics allows for more comfortable furniture and equipment, that is fine by me. The idea that it is necessary to prevent pain and disability is what is absurd.

So, why do people develop pain at their workplace? They do so for all of the reasons I've stated earlier. The pain is created by the brain as a strategy to keep us from thinking about and dealing with unpleasant thoughts and emotions. It is because of personality traits and stress in everyday life, and it is cumulative. The scene is further set if someone doesn't like their work, does not get along with colleagues or their supervisor or believes their work could result in pain and disability. The last sentiment refers again to conditioning; if a condition is **in vogue** it can be self-perpetuating. Just because something is commonly believed does not mean it is right. Trying to think differently and to get others to think differently is extremely difficult, akin to salmon swimming upstream, bucking the prevailing current. This is my goal, for I have seen the beneficial results with so

many.

Chapter 17

CHEST, SHOULDERS AND ELBOWS

Used to be that only professional baseball pitchers had shoulder surgery. Now it is an increasingly common procedure for the average Joe. Everyone with shoulder pain is diagnosed with rotator cuff tendonitis, impingement syndrome (a rotator cuff tendon pinched by the coracoid process, a bony protuberance on the scapula, or shoulder blade) or a torn labrum (cartilage tear). If medications, injections and physical therapy fail to help (as they often do – remember what happens when a physical modality is used to treat symptoms with a psychological cause?), surgery is offered. I see three major reasons for this. First, our medical system is providing more specialists, orthopedists or Sports Medicine orthopedists, who are trained to find physical and structural causes for physical symptoms. They receive little or no training that would inspire them to even contemplate a psychological cause. Second, there is widespread availability and routine use of the MRI. The MRI of the shoulder is a beautiful thing to behold; it reveals astounding detail, much like the MRI of the spine. But like the MRI of the spine, "abnormalities" are often incidental findings, not the cause of symptoms. Third, shoulder pain is now **in vogue**, like back pain, foot pain and reflux (more on this one later).

This is why so many continue to have pain, even after surgery. Some get temporary relief only (think placebo) and others develop the onset of a new pain shortly after (with TMS the brain moves the pain around, never giving up its strategy, wanting you to think, "Could it be physical instead of TMS?").

This is not to say that there aren't valid indications for surgery and good long-term results for some. Though I am obviously critical of physicians in these pages, they can do marvelous things for patients, in the right circumstances. Again, I'm a case in point. While road cycling in 1997, I took a spill at a relatively high speed and suffered significant trauma to my right shoulder and also broke my left wrist. Dr. Rob Swiggett was nice enough to put my shoulder back together and I'm now good as new. My point is that chronic, nagging, intermittent shoulder symptoms in the absence of significant trauma are more likely to have a psychological than a physical cause. Again, I must invoke, why the epidemic of shoulder pain and we cannot be so fragile!

Tennis elbow is another epidemic in the works and it's not just for tennis players anymore! Everyone is now fair game. Used to be the only ones with tennis elbow were those with bad backhands and wood racquets. The old wood racquets would vibrate more when the ball was improperly struck, the resulting force generating a very unpleasant sensation in the lateral elbow ("tennis elbow"). Now that racquets are lighter, make of remarkable space age materials and often employing vibration dampening, it is the rare tennis player with tennis elbow symptoms caused by the sport.

Tennis elbow's medical name is lateral epicondylitis, a type of tendonitis. The lateral epicondyle is where the tendon for the forearm extensor muscles inserts on the bone. This type of tendonitis may follow trauma or an overuse injury. A good example of the latter is when someone works intensely on a home improvement project over a weekend – reshingling the roof, putting up drywall or painting. As the muscles and tendons are not used to such an activity or so much time spent at the endeavor, an injury may occur. One of the beautiful things about our bodies is the ability to heal, so this pain should subside within days or, at the outside, several weeks. When this pain presents well outside the typical window of healing, it is essential to ask yourself, "What is going on?" Most practitioners and well-meaning friends will tell you that:

1) You must be re-injuring it.

2) You haven't rested it enough.

3) Sometimes these things can take months to heal.

Or: 4) Some other biomechanical condition exists.

What has actually occurred is that your brain has taken advantage of the situation and has allowed the pain to remain there, for if you believe reasons #1, 2, 3 or 4, you will be convinced there is a physical rather than a psychological cause for your symptoms. You will then pursue physical remedies, your pain will persist and your brain will have successfully created a distraction that will keep you from thinking about or dealing with unpleasant thoughts and emotions.

Does this sound familiar? I hope so, because it is only through repetition that you can undo the conditioning created by your past experiences and reprogram your mind to think differently about your body. This is the hard work, forgetting all that you've learned before and conditioning yourself to view the psychological-physical connection in this manner. It is this that will ultimately ease your pain.

Larry, 31 years old and married for the second time, had been diagnosed with bilateral carpal tunnel syndrome and lateral epicondylitis. He had elbow, forearm, wrist and hand pain of two years' duration that had failed to respond to rest, NSAIDs, wrist splints and forearm bands.

He admitted that his symptoms began with an increase in marital stress with his second wife. With children from both marriages, he acknowledges significant financial pressures as well as a desire to be a good father. His pain left shortly after our visit and he remains pain-free more than two years later.

Bill had elbow pain for more than one year when he came to me. He had seen an orthopedist and been treated with physical therapy,

NSAIDs and cortisone injections for lateral epicondylitis – all to no avail.

He had no problem identifying himself as a perfectionist preoccupied with his responsibilities as a husband and father. The cycles of his business were also a source of great stress.

Bill was able to eliminate his elbow symptoms quickly. When shoulder and chest pains then appeared to replace the elbow pain, appropriate studies were done. When all tests came back negative, he agreed TMS was again the culprit and has felt fine since.

Frank, married with two daughters, is in his 40's and has frequent episodes of chest pain. His first episode was associated with a viral infection of his heart, known as myocarditis. He had a complete recovery, yet for the past four or five years he experiences chest pain that is similar in nature to that which he experienced when diagnosed with myocarditis. He describes a constant ache that can last for days at a time and worries him greatly. Thorough cardiac evaluations have been done several times, all with normal findings.

He admits that he is "somewhat anxious" by nature. Devoted to his family, he also works two jobs. Always upbeat, he initially thinks it unlikely that stress could be to blame for his chest pain, but does warm to the concept. Free of chest pain for more than two years, he amusedly told me the pain had relocated to his elbow, but was now resolving with the use of knowledge.

Chapter 18

HIPS, KNEES AND LEGS

I'd like to start by stating that total hip joint replacement can be a miraculous surgery. However, just as CT scans and MRI studies of the spine show degenerative changes in most of us as we age (usually incidental and not the cause of symptoms), so, too, will hip x-rays often reveal degenerative changes that are not the cause of symptoms. This case proves this point.

Jack was a former athlete, now in his 40's, with left hip pain. His orthopedist told him that he would benefit from a new hip joint as his x-ray showed "significant" degenerative changes. After this visit his left hip pain increased and he mentioned it to me at the time of his annual physical exam. When he told me that his right hip felt fine, I asked him to humor me by having both of his hips x-rayed. On x-ray, both hips had the same "degenerative" changes, yet his right hip did not hurt! I advised him to put off surgery, resume activity (he had significantly decreased his exercise after being told of his arthritic condition) and not pay too much attention to his hips. Following these instructions, his discomfort subsided and he successfully resumed exercise and athletics.

I've had quite a few patients like Jack. Enough to recommend x-rays of both hips in all of my patients with complaints of chronic hip pain. Invariably both appear similar on x-ray, though only one will hurt. This is often sufficient to convince someone that they have TMS – that their very real physical pain has a psychological cause.

What is particularly interesting are the explanations offered by various practitioners when x-rays are normal. People are given elaborate explanations about biomechanics and told they have problems with various muscles (like the psoas), tendons (ITB, or iliotibial band) or bursae (bursitis). Sometimes they are told they have a knee problem that is resulting in hip pain. While this is possible, I believe it is far less common than generally claimed. Leg-length discrepancy is another condition that has been blamed for hip, knee or foot pain (and even back pain). I find this extremely amusing. Assuming that the patient's legs are the same as the set he was born with, that he has used these very same legs for all types of activities before without any problem, then why should this asymmetry be responsible for symptoms NOW? How does this make sense? That person's musculoskeletal system has never known differently – it is perfectly adapted to its structure.

TMS affecting the knees is also fairly easy to recognize. A significant physical process responsible for knee pain is invariably indicated by the history and examination. A sudden blow to the knee, a forceful twisting or acute hyperextension can cause damage to bone, cartilage or ligament. However, most of the chronic and episodic knee pain lacks this type of history and exam fails to reveal important intra-articular pathology. Eager to give a physical rationale for these chronic, intermittent symptoms, physicians will offer chondromalacia patella, patellofemoral syndrome, iliotibial band syndrome (ITB again), arthritis, bursitis, tendonitis or possibly a small cartilage injury not evident on exam. What all of these have in common is the presence of a chronic, non-healing process. Although we are incredible creations with a remarkable ability to heal, for some reason, we are told that there is an ongoing physical problem. So, a litany of physical remedies are prescribed: anti-inflammatory medication, steroid injections, braces and supports, glucosamine chondroitin (no better than placebo in my experience), physical therapy, special exercises to strengthen the quadriceps and possibly arthroscopy (surgery).

In my experience these physical remedies either fail or provide only temporary relief, supporting the notion of a placebo response. Not infrequently if pain subsides, pain will surface in a new area – the brain does not give up its strategy!

Lately I've noted an increasing frequency of lower leg pain, either in the calf or shin. Calf pain is described as sharp or stabbing and may be precipitated by certain weight-bearing activities, but not by others. The common diagnosis is muscle strain, pull or tear, though I've seen it explained as compartment syndrome (this is an unusual condition where exercise induces such an increase in blood flow and muscle swelling that the pressure within the muscle compartment becomes too great, resulting in pain). Usually the person has done adequate stretching and warm-up before the activity and the activity itself is not unusually strenuous or unreasonable for the given level of fitness. I know this one from personal experience because this is what my brain hit me with after I eliminated my back pain and sciatica. Want to hear ridiculous? I could walk without much difficulty – if I tried to jog, I'd get intense pain after 50 yards! I could bicycle 50 miles or do one hour on the Nordic Track, but I couldn't run 100 yards! After many vociferous discussions with my brain, I was able to get rid of this pain and have run five marathons in the past three years.

Pain in the anterior lower leg, or shin, can be described as dull, aching or sometimes sharp. Diagnoses may include muscle strain, shin splints or stress fracture.

X-rays or bone scans may be used to support these diagnoses. Despite this, I have found that TMS is the most common culprit. Again, I will acknowledge that we can get injured, particularly if we do a new activity to excess or improperly. However, the typical individual with shin pain will have appropriate footwear and gear, they will be doing appropriate stretching and warm-up, and they will be doing an activity that they have been doing regularly, with facility and expertise. So, why do they get pain now? Once I point this out, most will accept TMS and be able to get rid of their pain and resume exercise. This is an exemplary case:

Steven is a teenager and a budding running phenom. In the course of his training he began to experience left shin pain. He had not suddenly increased his mileage or suffered any trauma. Methodical in all things, his footwear, nutrition and hydration are all appropriate. Podiatrist and orthopedist recommend rest as treatment for presumed stress fracture. When he returns to running the pain returns. A bone scan is ordered and interpreted as showing a stress fracture and more rest is advised. At this point he came to see me. He admitted to being a perfectionist and putting much pressure on himself. Not surprisingly he's a straight A student and participates in a host of extracurricular activities in addition to running. After I explained why I think his leg pain is psychological and running should not cause him pain, he went home and read **The Mindbody Prescription**. The *next afternoon* he phoned, obviously very excited. He had just returned from a long run and felt fine! He went on to have an outstanding season, continually lowering his times and improving his performance. His only frustration was an inability to convince his teammates to think psychological and better deal with their "injuries."

Barbara came in for evaluation of chronic hip pain. She also noted intermittent heel, knee and low back pain. Symptoms appeared to have begun around the time of her mother's illness and death several years prior. She worked full time in addition to her responsibilities at home to her husband and teenagers.

She admitted to self-esteem issues and was candid about growing up in an environment with multiple alcoholic family members. Her pain vanished and has not returned since she learned that it was psychologically caused.

Chapter 19

FEET

Feet are a favorite topic of mine right now. There is a veritable epidemic of foot pain in our society. All of a sudden, everyone has foot problems, from pro athletes to the couch potato next door. This has not always been the case. Think hard, back 10 to 20 years ago. Do you remember hearing so much about plantar fasciitis, heel spurs, and other foot disorders? Of course you don't, because foot pain was relatively uncommon then. When I started my medical training about 20 years ago, foot pain was not a common complaint, now it is in vogue and everywhere you turn.

There is no doubt in my mind that the overwhelming majority of foot pain attributed to plantar fasciitis, heel spurs, neuromas, or other physical causes is TMS. Here is something to think about: why should the incidence of foot pain be increasing now? It makes no sense. WE are not strolling about on rocky, uneven trails, barefoot, like our ancestors did. We are not shod in rudimentary footwear, lacking cushion or support. In fact, I would argue that the footwear industry has done an incredible job providing us with supremely comfortable and affordable shoes. Not only is there a vast array of styles, but we have shoes specifically designed for every waking activity. There are shoes for walking, running, hiking, cross-training, aerobics, tennis, soccer, baseball, football, squash, racquetball, bicycling, rock climbing, golf, basketball – the list goes on. There are shoes in different widths, for overpronators or underpronators, for heavier folks, or those who are lighter, for high arches or low arches, for those who prefer extra cushioning or a wider toe box. The choices are dazzling. Now people are getting foot pain? How does this make sense at all?

Most of us have been upright, standing, walking, running, skipping, climbing since the age of one year. Suddenly our feet should start to hurt? This makes no sense. Falling from a significant height and landing on our feet – that should cause pain. But even in that scenario, with trauma, we heal (unless the trauma is severe) promptly and the pain leaves. Even broken bones heal, within four to eight weeks, except for truly extraordinary circumstances.

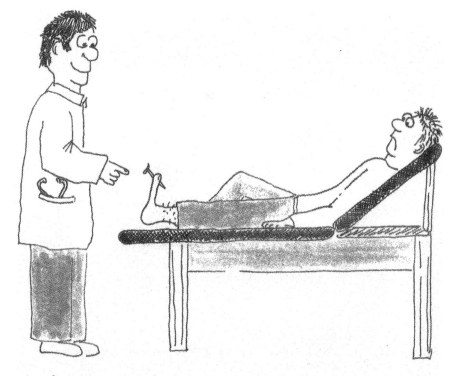

"NOW THIS WOULD EXPLAIN WHY YOUR FOOT HURTS."

Yet, well-meaning orthopedists and podiatrists will provide a detailed lecture on foot mechanics and a very convincing explanation of the suddenly acquired physical inadequacies responsible for the pain. Why? Because this is what they are taught: a physical symptom must have a physical cause. Yes, we all can get injured. Step in a hole and you may sprain your ankle, injuring ligaments. But this heals. We are fantastic creatures, as I'll remind you often. We have an amazing capacity to heal quickly when injured. When pain and discomfort linger well beyond the timeframe for expected healing following an injury, what is going on? Have we suddenly become defective, losing our innate ability to heal? If pain develops and stays without obvious trauma or an unusual physical stress, what's going on there? How does that make sense? And if that discomfort becomes chronic, then logic has really been defied. We cannot be so fragile. If so, how could we still exist? We'd be extinct, having been wiped off the face of the earth as a result of being so feeble in the face of normal activities.

So now, foot pain is in vogue. It is acceptable. Everyone has it. The pain, the nuisance, serves as a distraction, keeping unpleasant thoughts and emotions at bay. It is fine to commiserate with others about aching feet, far more acceptable than ranting and raving about stressful issues in your life, past or present.

Complain enough and your feet will get injected, put in splints or fit for orthotics.

Undoubtedly medication will be prescribed. Maybe you'll eventually have surgery. Even worse than those treatments will be the inevitable advice to stop running or quit aerobics class, to get off your feet. Exercise, which helps to maintain conditioning and fitness, aid with stress management and even improve mood, will be taken away in the name of modern medicine. Not too difficult to imagine the consequences, is it?

Oh, yes, sometimes the pain seems improved with one of these therapies. However, in my experience, the relief may be temporary, as with any placebo response (Remember, very few people really want to be in pain). If it appears to last longer, it is inevitable that a new pain will surface at another location. This is the brain's strategy, to make you believe that the cause is physical, rather than psychological, and to keep you guessing, off-balance.

As an aside, I think the foot pain epidemic began shortly after Larry Bird's surgery for heel spurs in the early 1980's. Heel spurs are often incidental findings on foot x-rays, but now are regularly blamed for foot pain. Which leads to the question: were heel spurs to blame for Larry Bird's foot pain? Obviously, I cannot answer that, but in the chapter on athletes I postulate how a competitive athlete's personality makes him/her a set-up for TMS.

Jack is a 45-year-old with heel and foot pain for more than one year. Diagnosed by both a podiatrist and orthopedist as having plantar fasciitis, nothing has alleviated his daily foot pain. He's tried orthotics, NSAIDs, taping, stretching and special exercises to no avail. In addition to his foot pain, he has a history of chronic intermittent back pain despite two surgeries, reflux, migraines and irritable bowel syndrome.

Married with two children, he is self-employed and trying to get a book published. He is very happy with his life but acknowledges that he feels much responsibility for his family and realizes that this is a source of stress.

At my urging he stopped all treatments and within two weeks his foot pain resolved. His other symptoms have also improved.

Chapter 20

FIBROMYALGIA

People who have been told they have fibromyalgia (FMS) will either be elated after reading this or completely irate. Don't misunderstand me, these people are truly suffering. They may experience constant pain in multiple locations, or intermittent pain, but they are in pain. All have been through comprehensive evaluations that fail to reveal another etiology. There are symptom checklists that assist physicians in applying this diagnosis and there are often concomitant mood disorders, such as depression and anxiety. A lot of discussion has centered on whether the mood disorder comes first and then is to blame for the physical symptoms, a true "chicken or egg" conundrum. On the other hand, how would your mood be if you were often in pain?

There are no successful treatment options. Oh, many things are tried, but none succeed. To add further insult to injury, everyone is invariably told they have to live with it. This is how the traditional, mainstream medical establishment chooses to deal with it.

But the answer is right here. There can be no doubt that the disorder known as fibromyalgia is really a severe form of TMS. As such, it will respond to this approach, but progress can be slow. The reason for this is that these sufferers have been deeply ingrained with their diagnosis through their experience with traditional as well as alternative medical providers. They believe they have a physical problem, not a psychological one, only the powers that be have yet to identify the causative agent or process. They may receive disability compensation for it (though I do believe most would gladly trade their pain for the checks). They go through an endless parade of remedies – wouldn't you be willing to try anything? Many participate in support groups. All of this reinforces the notion of a physically, rather than psychologically, based disorder. It is all conditioning and the sheer magnitude of it is responsible for making it difficult to lick, even when recognized as TMS; but I have helped those with FMS – even a handful of success stories is confirmation that FMS is TMS, because NOTHING ELSE WORKS.

Renee is a woman in her 40's with diffuse myalgias and a multitude of other unpleasant symptoms for more than four years. Diagnosed with fibromyalgia, she described shooting pains in her head, pain in her neck, hips, shoulders, pelvis, arms and back that could be experienced as sharp, aching or burning. She also described numbness in her forearms and fingers with keyboard work. For much of this time she also had ear and jaw pain and for the previous six months complained of intermittent nausea, dizziness, and a sense of being off-balance. Along the way she had also been diagnosed with TMJ, carpal tunnel syndrome, irritable bowel syndrome and reflux. A family physician, neurologist, ear, nose and throat specialist, dentist, oral surgeon and allergist had evaluated her. Every test, including exhaustive blood tests and imaging studies, was normal. She had tried everything but the kitchen sink – antidepressant medication, dental appliance, chiropractic, etc. She had been in counseling for years.

After I explained that she had a severe form of TMS, not fibromyalgia, she revealed a personal warehouse of stress that was enormous. Married with four children, she also worked full time as a teacher. Her mother had died suddenly from a cerebral hemorrhage. Her father had died following a long difficult struggle with multiple sclerosis. One of her sisters had been diagnosed with multiple sclerosis. Another sister was suffering from depression. Within two months of our initial meeting her symptoms were gone and have not returned.

Chapter 21

CHRONIC FATIGUE SYNDROME

This will be another short chapter. Chronic fatigue syndrome (CFS) has much in common with all of the other manifestations of **The Mindbody Syndrome**, like FMS, low back pain, neck and shoulder pain, etc. In this case the persistent unpleasant symptom is fatigue, often to the point of disability. Nothing is found on comprehensive medical evaluation, though people often have associated mood disorders. A joint commission of three of Britain's Royal Medical Colleges concluded, after a comprehensive study a few years ago, that CFS was probably psychologically induced. It is clearly another manifestation of TMS, most likely initiated by dysfunctional activity in the neuroendocrine system. Therefore, one can anticipate resolution of symptoms by treating it the same way as one treats TMS. Again, it will be very hard work, for many of the same reasons that treating FMS can be challenging

In a personal correspondence, Dr. Sarno wrote that a group of young men and women had read one of his books, decided that the psychology of CFS was similar to that of TMS, and got better.

Chapter 22

AN UPSET STOMACH – BEYOND ULCERS; IRRITABLE

BOWEL SYNDROME, REFLUX AND DYSPEPSIA

Yes, people still get ulcers, but the incidence has declined thanks

to H2-blockers (medication) and the fact that gastroesophageal reflux

disease (GERD, or simply "reflux") is now in vogue. When ulcers

were in their heyday, most acknowledged the role of stress in their

formation. Not so with GERD, thus creating fertile ground for its

ascendance. The most common symptom of GERD is heartburn and

the H2-blockers that worked so well for ulcers don't work so well for

this. That is why Prilosec (a proton pump inhibitor) is now the #1

selling medication in the world. If you had doubts about the epidemic

status of GERD, this fact alone should take care of that.

Unfortunately the managed care companies are a little slow on the

uptake and often refuse to fill prescriptions for proton pump

inhibitors, insisting we prescribe H2-blockers, a much lower cost medication. With GERD, the acidic stomach contents reflux or regurgitate back up the esophagus. This is not pleasant or desirable. The lining of the esophagus is not meant to tolerate the low pH of the gastric material; thus, it can cause burning or other painful sensations (it is, after all, acid) when contacting the esophagus. Ordinarily, the lower esophageal sphincter (LES), a muscular band at the junction of the esophagus and stomach, remains closed after the ingestion of food or fluids. A closed LES prevents reflux. There are certain substances that can allow the LES to relax (or open) – alcohol, caffeine and nicotine – as well as certain medications. There is also no doubt that an overly full stomach, causing gastric distention, can result in increased pressure that overwhelms the LES. This effect can be magnified by laying down with an overly full stomach.

However, GERD symptoms often persist even when the obvious accommodations to the above information are made. So, what is going on? From my experience, in this situation psychic factors are affecting the LES.

Why am I convinced that GERD is part of TMS, a mindbody disorder? Well, when I began my medical training nearly 20 years ago, GERD was not a common disorder. Over the past 10 years the incidence of it has skyrocketed, hence the boom in sales for Prilosec and its cousins. GERD is the 2000's answer to the ulcers of the 1960's and the 1970's. I have had many patients eliminate their reflux symptoms when they recognize it as psychologically induced.

Dyspepsia, also known as nonulcer dyspepsia, is another upper gastrointestinal tract disorder. Symptoms may include upper abdominal bloating, fullness, cramping or "gassiness." Sometimes it is made worse by meals, other times better. Work-up fails to reveal an ulcer, GERD or other physical process, hence the name, which is really just a description of the symptoms. Nothing helps reliably, not H2-blockers, antacids or proton pump inhibitors. What does this tell you? What I think is that this will be the next upper GI disorder to become epidemic. I presume the pharmaceutical industry is hard at work . . .

Irritable bowel syndrome (IBS) is the reincarnation of "spastic colon." The good news here is that many physicians believe that there is a psychological component; the bad news is that they don't know how to teach their patients to address the psychological cause.

It's not about stress management or positive thinking. It's about understanding how psychology can affect physiology – how lower abdominal cramps, bloating, gassiness and diarrhea or constipation are all symptoms created as a distraction. Focused on the bowels, an individual cannot then contemplate those unpleasant things stashed in the unconscious.

IBS sufferers, like those with FMS and CFS, often have a thorough evaluation (perhaps including a colonoscopy – a procedure in which a 140 centimeter fiberoptic tube is introduced through the rectum and can visualize the entire colon, or large intestine) that fails to reveal a physical process. Good advice includes plenty of exercise, increasing intake of fiber-containing foods and water – hey, that's smart for anyone. Unfortunately, symptoms usually persist until IBS is recognized as TMS and treated as such.

Bonnie is a 33-year-old married woman with severe low back pain that developed after a complicated pregnancy. Pain could travel into either leg and she also described intermittent pains at other locations, sometimes severe. She was told that her symptoms were due to leg-length discrepancy as well as multilevel disc disease, diagnosed on MRI.

When she saw me, she had failed all traditional therapies and was fearful that she would be unable to care for her child or return to work (as she desired). In retrospect, she identified her history of panic attacks, irritable bowel syndrome and previous episodes of back pain and paresthesias more than ten years prior as earlier manifestations of TMS.

She gave up her lift (meant to treat the leg length discrepancy) and was much better within several months. Three years later she contacted me to provide an update – not only was she feeling well, but the irritable bowel symptoms that had plagued her for fourteen years were gone too.

Chapter 23

SKIN DEEP - ECZEMA , PSORIASIS and URTICARIA

The link between stress and certain dermatologic disorders is well established. The most common chronic skin conditions with this association are eczema, psoriasis and urticaria (hives). All cause pruritus, or itching, and can involve any part of the body surface. Pruritus can range from mild to severe and can occur intermittently or be constant. While itching may not be pain, when it is severe it is not only as distracting as pain, it can drive someone insane. There are medications, oral and topical, that can help, but they do not always reduce symptoms.

Sometimes there is an obvious precipitant, some substance responsible for the rash. When the substance is withdrawn or avoided, the rash may clear. Unfortunately there is not usually an identifiable physical precipitant. This has led to the awareness of stress and psychological factors being responsible for these disorders.

I have had patients inform me that their particular itchy skin condition resolved when they successfully employed TMS principles to eliminate their pain. I have also had patients who directed their efforts primarily at their skin condition as TMS with resolution of their rash and reduction in recurrence rate.

Chapter 24

HITTING BELOW THE BELT – GENITOURINARY

COMPLAINTS

By now you've figured out that TMS can result in pain or discomfort virtually anywhere. There are those who suffer from pain in the genital region. In men, chronic symptoms involving the testicles, scrotum, prostate, bladder and urethra (the tube through which urine passes from the bladder out through the penis) often receive diagnoses like chronic epididymitis, prostatodynia, interstitial cystitis, chronic urethritis and sometimes even herniated disc! Women with chronic complaints may be told they have vulvodynia, interstitial cystitis, chronic urethritis or irritable bowel syndrome. Sometimes pelvic pain is ascribed to endometriosis or ovarian cysts, though these are often incidental findings and not a cause for pain.

In each case, comprehensive medical evaluation fails to turn up a cause for the complaint. Not too surprisingly, symptoms usually persist despite a wide array of remedies, traditional or alternative. The best results I've seen are when patients accept that their physical symptoms have a psychological cause.

Matt, an attorney in his 30's, had previously been diagnosed with chronic epididymitis. He would have frequent episodes of testicular pain. Physical exam and tests were always unrevealing. Antibiotics and NSAIDs did not help. When without testicular symptoms, he often experienced palpitations, tinnitus, elbow pain diagnosed as lateral epicondylitis and diffuse gastrointestinal symptoms labeled irritable bowel syndrome.

Easily able to identify perfectionist and goodist tendencies, he quickly embraced TMS thinking and has been fine since.

Chapter 25

MORE ABOVE THE NECK

There are some other pain syndromes or disorders causing other unpleasant symptoms that involve the face, mouth and ears. I believe all are TMS for they share certain features with TMS elsewhere in the body:

1) Thorough medical evaluation fails to identify a significant cause;

2) Treatment is unsuccessful;

3) Symptoms are chronic, either persistent or intermittent;

4) Symptoms are intrusive, providing distraction;

5) Symptoms resolve with TMS treatment.

TRIGEMINAL NEURALGIA

Of those that I have encountered, the most bothersome and disabling is trigeminal neuralgia, also known as tic doloreaux. The trigeminal or fifth cranial nerve provides sensation to areas of the face and teeth. With this disorder, patients experience brief episodes of intense facial pain that may be described as sharp, stabbing or burning. These episodes may recur over any time frame, causing misery for the sufferer. Particularly puzzling is that precipitants seem to include formerly benign actions, like opening the mouth, touching the face, brushing teeth, etc. If ever a problem seemed to have a psychological rather than physical basis, this is it. No physical cause has been identified and various medications, injections and surgical procedures rarely provide more than temporary relief. Some become so despondent that they contemplate suicide. I've seen patients with pain so severe they require hospital admission and administration of intravenous morphine by patient-controlled analgesia (PCA), with only partial relief despite extremely high doses of the narcotic.

Fortunately, trigeminal neuralgia is not common. I've had success treating this and this case is illustrative. Janet had classic symptoms of trigeminal neuralgia for several years when I first saw her. Prior care for this had been with another family physician, neurologist, and neurosurgeon. Oral medications including anticonvulsants (typically used to treat seizure disorders, but often used for neuropathic pain syndromes), steroids, non-steroidal anti-inflammatory drugs (NSAIDs) and narcotics had been prescribed. Injections and surgical procedures involving the nerve failed. She was on high doses of narcotics at her first visit with me, and acknowledged escalating usage. Like many at first hearing of TMS, she was skeptical. Desperate for help, she put aside her reluctance and read **The Mindbody Prescription** by Dr. John Sarno and recognized herself in those pages. Married with two small children, she was forced to work outside of the home due to financial pressures. She acknowledged a childhood that was at times very difficult and had little relationship with her father. I helped her to wean off the narcotics and she has remained pain-free for more than five years now.

MOUTH

TMJ

Temporomandibular joint syndrome (TMJ) is pain that occurs at the angle of the jaw, where the mandible (lower jaw bone) meets the temporal bone. It is a hinge type of joint (like the elbow) and is used for any activity that involves opening the mouth. Like any joint, injury can result from trauma. Like any joint, healing should occur within a brief time frame. Some cases of TMJ may be caused by excessive teeth grinding (bruxism) or jaw-clenching during sleep, which certainly qualifies as a type of dental trauma. Most dentists recognize that stress is the cause for bruxism and jaw clenching and share this with patients with routine success. Some do use a dental appliance for a short time, but can discard it eventually. My experience is that TMJ resolves most quickly when a psychological cause is accepted.

BMS

You may not have heard of burning mouth syndrome (BMS) yet, but I have no doubt that you will. It is gathering steam and I have no doubt that it is a disorder with a psychological cause. The chief complaint is of a burning sensation in the mouth, but some also complain of a bitter or metallic taste. As with many TMS equivalents, no cause is identified and treatment is infrequently successful. The most commonly prescribed medication is a benzodiazepine, like Klonopin. Any time that you learn that a benzodiazepine is prescribed for a disorder, your radar should go up and you should think "TMS" and psychological cause. Klonopin and its cousins are tranquilizers, sedating substances that can cause relaxation and reduce feelings of stress; unfortunately they do not fix the problem, provide only temporary relief and can quickly become habit-forming, no matter the reason for the original prescription.

EARS

TINNITUS, HYPERACUSIS, VERTIGO

The audiovestibular or eighth cranial nerve is involved with hearing ("audio" component) and balance ("vestibular" component, part of the inner ear which is the body's internal gyroscope). When affected by TMS, symptoms may include ringing in the ears (tinnitus), unusual sensitivity to sound (hyperacusis) and/or intermittent dizziness (vertigo). If there is no history of significant noise exposure or physical trauma, and traditional medical evaluation (including imaging study, such as MRI or CT scan) fails to reveal obvious pathology, TMS may be the culprit. Again, it is a situation where physical symptoms become intrusive and provide distraction, unresponsive to traditional remedies.

While only a handful of patients have seen me primarily for these type of symptoms, I have had quite a few tell me their symptoms resolved when they successfully attacked other TMS complaints. It is easy to hear critics cry: "Anecdotal evidence! This is not scientific!"

I would argue that when you start to string together a lot of "anecdotes," it is worth paying attention.

Chapter 26

RESTLESS LEGS

Restless leg syndrome (RLS) is another unpleasant condition that seems to be increasing in frequency. It is characterized by an uncomfortable sensation in the legs that can only be relieved by moving the legs. Some describe it as a crawling, tingling, aching or itching sensation. If not a side effect of another medication, RLS evaluation rarely turns up a cause. Once more, various medications, including benzodiazepines, anticonvulsants, narcotics and others, have been tried with unsatisfactory results. If a cause is not identified, I encourage RLS sufferers to try "thinking psychological." I have had patients successfully eliminate their RLS with this approach.

Chapter 27

ATHLETES

Doesn't it seem that pro athletes are spending more and more time on the disabled list? On injured reserve? Does the sports page read more like the chatter at a family reunion, noting who is suffering from what and who has had surgery recently? Does this make sense to you? It doesn't make sense to me.

Today's athletes have access to better training, better nutrition, and more information about optimizing performance than ever before. Why does it seem they are dropping like flies? No doubt certain sports involve collisions that can cause serious trauma. Clearly, this is not what I'm referring to when I point out the skyrocketing incidence of muscle strains, tendonitis, bursitis, etc. The better someone's fitness or conditioning, the less susceptible they should be to injury. So, why should someone develop pain doing an activity they have done extensively and proficiently before?

This pain is real. No doubt the athlete does not wish to have pain, or see his performance hindered. Well, the competitive athlete is no different than the non-athlete, at least with respect to the machinations of the brain. Again, pain is created as a distraction, to keep unpleasant thoughts and emotions in the unconscious. Based on my experience working with athletes, I'd argue that they possess greater perfectionist tendencies and so put even greater pressure on themselves. This self-imposed pressure to perform and succeed adds to the reservoir of stress and rage.

Marathon training serves as an excellent example – something I can speak to from both personal and professional experience. Training for an endurance event requires a tremendous amount of discipline. It is essential to meticulously plan time for training, nutrition, hydration, equipment, and clothing appropriate for weather conditions. Add to this the self-imposed pressure to achieve a certain goal or time and you've got excellent material for the creation of TMS. I believe that pain attributed to "overuse" or "overtraining" is almost always TMS. This goes back to the notion that we are somehow fragile and incapable of maintaining certain levels of physical activity. What is occurring is that the brain utilizes the activity (running, in this case) as a trigger for the creation of pain. It is successful if we buy in to the idea of "overuse," that has been promulgated by the medical mainstream. That is an example of **conditioning** – we are told, and then come to believe, that "overuse" occurs – that the pain is to be expected and accepted as a result of the activity.

My experience preparing for and at the 2001 Boston Marathon provides an example. As mentioned earlier in the book, I was able to eliminate chronic low back pain and sciatica using Dr. Sarno's advice. Success doesn't mean the brain relinquishes its' strategy, and so searing calf pain developed one month before the marathon. The pain would come on only several hundred yards into my run. Disconsolate, I would limp home, all the while yelling (internally) at my brain. I could walk. I could bicycle 50 miles. I simply could not run more than a hundred yards without the acute onset of stabbing pain. Increasing the amount of time each day spent reflecting, I tried to maintain my fitness by bicycling and exercising on a Nordic Track. Having never run Boston, but hearing nothing but great tales from friends who had, I was determined to try. Anxious that the pain would recur and that I'd fail, I asked my family not to attend. Gingerly I started out and was giddy when I got beyond 500 yards without pain. So far, so good. Then, at mile six, it hit. I screamed silently, telling my brain that there was no physical reason for the pain and that I would not allow it to continue. I acknowledged my perfectionism, compulsive traits, and other foibles. I reminded myself of worries I harbor about my family, my children. The pain left. I completed the marathon, far slower than hoped, but not too poorly considering the lack of running in the month prior.

Kevin's tale is similar, but even more impressive as he was able to complete an Ironman Triathlon. He was training for his first Ironman competition when he developed left hip and leg pain just one month before the event. The Ironman is a remarkable endurance event. The Ironman is a remarkable endurance event, requiring participants to swim 2.4 miles, bicycle 112 miles (without drafting) and to finish, run a marathon (26.2 miles).

A veteran of marathons and triathlons, Kevin's pain began when he decreased his training as part of the pre-event taper recommended for this type of competition. Given the incredible amount of training and commitment this required, he was extremely upset about the possibility that he'd be unable to participate. Fortunately he recognized that his pain could be TMS. Kevin shared with me that he had successfully eliminated low back pain, shoulder pain, and leg pain, the last diagnosed as ITB syndrome, by reading and re-reading Dr. Sarno's books over the past five years. Given how meticulous he was with training and how superbly conditioned he was, he agreed it made no sense that he should have suddenly developed a physical problem.

A week before the Ironman he then developed low back and groin pain. I offered him advice on how to conquer his pain and encouraged him to at least start the race. He was in discomfort when he started, but his pain faded and he told me that he was absolutely fine by the end of the race. He said, "Thank you again for your help! I feel extremely fortunate to have been able to finish (he did better than just finish – he achieved an excellent time). It pains me to see so many friends battling TMS-like ailments."

So, the professional athlete, like the amateur, has self-imposed pressure to perform. But he also has enormous pressure from the public. Often paid exorbitant sums to compete, today's athlete faces greater scrutiny from fans and the press. This is not to elicit sympathy by any means, but to offer information that could be used to help athletes remain healthy. Sports psychology should include TMS theory; I am confident it would help to improve performance and limit "injuries."

Chapter 28

EXCUSES, EXCUSES . . .

I cannot begin to tell you how many times someone has said to me, "I can't run because my knees hurt when I do." Actually, you could simply fill in the blanks: "I can't _____ (type of exercise or activity), because my _____ (name of body part) hurts when I do." Sound familiar? If you've read this far, you might recognize that this sounds a bit unlikely. Familiar themes should be echoing through your mind. If you're beginning to think outside of the box, your thought may be, "That doesn't make sense. Why should Bob* (name changed to protect the innocent) have pain in his knees when he runs? Is he suddenly so fragile? For his entire life until recently he could stand upright, walk, run, skip, and hop, and now this part of his body has failed him?" Have you ever wondered why so many golfers have back pain? Golf requires a fair amount of discipline and perfection, and in golf you do not really have an opponent—you are the opponent and you are playing against yourself.

Yes, there are certain physical conditions that could be responsible, but they are far less common causes of pain than you would believe. Yes, we can get injured, but we also have the capacity to heal well and quickly.

Unfortunately, the various medical personnel that you encounter will speak of "degenerative joint disease," "degenerative changes," "tendonitis," "bursitis," "leg length discrepancy," problems with your "biomechanics," problems with arches that are too high or too low, and on it goes. Imaging studies will be interpreted to support these explanations, despite the fact that many studies have confirmed that x-ray, CT, and MRI findings are frequently incidental, showing normal age-related changes and not the cause of symptoms. This contributes to us being conditioned to expect pain when we do that activity (remember, the activity is not really the cause, but a **trigger**).

Adding to this is the fact that everyone you know will support this mistaken belief. Your neighbors, co-workers, and tennis partners have had similar symptoms in the past and share with you, unsolicited of course, their own experience. Articles in newspapers and magazines, information on websites and television programs bombard us ceaselessly with similar information. There is no relief from the onslaught. If it is common, it if is *in vogue*, you will hear about it and the conditioning goes on.

Undoing the conditioning, re-programming your mind to think differently is not easy. It is no different than changing any longstanding habit. It's tough. Look how hard it is for most smokers to give up cigarettes. We all know alcoholics – we see how they struggle to abstain. It takes the ability to step outside of the box and begin to think differently about your body.

If you've played a certain sport or done a certain activity regularly, why should it now cause discomfort? I am not referring to the muscle soreness or fatigue that comes with exercise and activity; that is to be expected and resolves quickly in time or with improved fitness or more "practice." I am referring to chronic, longer-lasting symptoms. If you are presented with an "abnormality" on an x-ray, CT scan, or MRI, the chances are very good that the "abnormality" has been present for a long time. So, then why is the pain here now? Why didn't the pain begin earlier?

Asking these questions means you're on the way to getting rid of your pain.

Chapter 29

MOOD DISORDERS

I have had many patients who found that their mood disorders improved or resolved when they tackled their particular TMS symptoms. Anxiety disorders, such as obsessive-compulsive disorder (OCD), panic attacks, phobias and generalized anxiety disorder (GAD) seem to be the most responsive to this approach. As most are aware, these conditions result not only in feeling anxious or nervous, but are often coupled with unpleasant physical symptoms – very real physical symptoms that have a psychological cause. Commonly experienced symptoms include:

1) Palpitations

2) Chest pain

3) Shortness of breath

4) Sensation of choking

5) Sweating

6) Shaking or trembling

7) Dizziness or lightheadedness

8) Nausea

9) Abdominal discomfort (i.e., bloating, cramps)

10) Numbness or tingling

11) Chills

12) Hot flashes

With OCD, people experience repetitive intrusive thoughts (obsessions), which may result in performance of repetitive actions (compulsions, such as handwashing, checking, etc.). These physical symptoms and pervasive thoughts serve a common purpose – they provide a DISTRACTION. Instead of back pain, those with anxiety disorders have these unpleasant sensations. It all serves the same purpose, keeping the contents of the reservoir of rage in the unconscious.

Because of these successful results, I have introduced patients with these anxiety disorders to this approach with encouraging results. I must note that certain medications, like SSRIs (such as Prozac, Paxil, Zoloft, etc.) and TCAs (amitriptyline, imipramine, etc.) may also help. It is this type of finding that makes me suspect the physiology of TMS includes not only oxygen deprivation, but also primary neurochemical changes. In this case, relative reduction in serotonin, a neurochemical, is associated with symptoms of depression and anxiety. When serotonin levels are raised, symptoms improve.

I am sure some of you are wondering why I did not mention benzodiazepines (Xanax, Ativan, Klonopin, Valium, etc.), medications frequently prescribed for treatment of anxiety disorders. It is my opinion that they are overprescribed and have the potential to do great harm. They are extremely addictive, both physically and psychologically, and have great potential for abuse. More importantly, they cannot cure symptoms or heal the underlying problem. Benzodiazepines can only mask symptoms, providing temporary relief. They are all sedating and thus will interfere with cognition and motor skills and potentially impair judgment.

However, in my experience those reliant on medication often experience return of their mood disorder when medication is discontinued. Those who have applied TMS principles fare better. I think this helps explain a common concern regarding counseling and psychotherapy. First, I must opine that we could all benefit from psychotherapy, independent of physical symptoms or our emotional state. We could all learn to be better people, to handle stress better and abide by the golden rule. But therapy alone will not help to eliminate discomfort, be it physical or emotional. There must be **accurate thinking** as well, incorporation of TMS philosophy. It is necessary to understand <u>and</u> accept how psychology affects physiology. This explains why so many tell me that they have been in counseling, some for more than 30 years, and cannot understand why, if their symptoms have a psychological cause, they have not resolved.

This is further proof that getting better requires understanding and acceptance of TMS. It is not sufficient to resolve stressful issues, think positively or make major life changes, nor is it even necessary. Most will find this to be a relief. This does not mean you should jettison your therapist. As I said, counseling can be helpful for many reasons; however, it is not the solution.

If you have a good relationship with your therapist and find your sessions to be helpful, you might consider sharing TMS concepts with him/her. I have found psychologists and other therapists to be more open to this way of thinking than physicians. It could further enhance the value of therapy.

Chapter 30

SO WHAT DO I DO NOW? (OR, LET'S GET

PSYCHOLOGICAL)

OK. You've read this far and now are wondering, "what now?" It is surprisingly simple, even deceptively so, yet it can be very hard work. The first thing you have to do is forget everything you have ever been told about your body. Forget whatever diagnosis you have been given before. Forget all of the well-meaning advice you've been given by physicians, other practitioners, friends and family. Forget what you've read in magazines, newspapers and other self-help books. Put all of it aside. See, it's not so easy, but it is essential to getting better. You must undo all of the conditioning that has you believing in a physical or structural process responsible for your symptoms.

While you are contemplating the previous paragraph and before I go any further, another point bears mentioning. This is integral to re-programming your mind, to thinking differently. Attacking your

TMS symptoms *does not require positive thinking*. While it is good

to think positively and have an optimistic outlook with regard to your

self and life in general, it is not positive thinking that will cause

symptom resolution. If so, most of you would not be reading this. If

so, there would not be an epidemic of mindbody disorders. How do I

know this? Virtually everyone <u>wants</u> to be well. It is the rare

individual who wishes to experience pain and suffering. Most people

try very hard to ignore their symptoms, to soldier on. They try to

think positively; they try to put "mind over matter." In one form or

another, this is what most self-help books promote. Think positively,

just do it, mind over matter are common themes. Others focus on

stress management, behavioral modification and relaxation

techniques. Don't get me wrong; these are great skills to have.

Undoubtedly we could all do better with stress management and could

benefit from honing these skills. However, this is not what will

eliminate your pain. It doesn't require positive thinking. It requires

ACCURATE THINKING. Accurate thinking means understanding how psychological factors affect our physiology. Only when this exists can we truly heal ourselves.

Forgetting all that you have been told, in essence creating a new belief system, is extremely difficult. There are many obstacles, both within and without. Many people speak to me about fear. Invariably each has undergone a comprehensive evaluation by their physician (or multiple physicians). They may have been told they have one of the diagnoses that I have mentioned here. Very possibly they have been told that they must avoid certain activities or they will risk further damage or escalation of symptoms. For many this can be devastating, particularly if they have been advised to give up or curtail an activity that has brought them much pleasure. I have dealt with runners, cyclists, tennis players, hikers, etc., who were despondent about giving up or reducing their form of exercise. Even when they say they believe TMS is their problem and I've told them to resume exercise, they admit to being fearful that their symptoms will recur or increase. Fear is powerful and it is part of the conditioning that has occurred over time. It takes courage to put aside the fear.

Even when someone tells me they have gone ahead and done their activity with minimal or no pain, they may admit that they remain nervous or fearful about the next time. In many cases this may be a reflection of personality, as well as previous conditioning that needs to be undone. Remember, many with TMS are prone to worrying – they may be perfectionists, placing much pressure on themselves to do well, succeed or be well thought of, or they may be concerned about their ability to care for, or do for others. They may also have a more simple fear that their symptoms represent a physical decline or deterioration that heralds future morbidity or mortality.

So, when someone confronts their fear, does the activity and feels fine, I tell them to celebrate. **CELEBRATE!** I tell them to talk to their brain – tell themselves that they are fine! There cannot be a physical problem if they were able to do the activity without difficulty. Celebrating is an important way to re-program the mind. It is conditioning yourself to think differently about your body and will help you immeasurably to undo the old conditioning. It will help you to forget all that came before.

CELEBRATE!

On the flip side, it is important not to be discouraged if symptoms arise during the course of an activity. It simply means that more mental work must be done. It is easy for fear and its compatriot, doubt, to creep in. "Maybe it isn't TMS, maybe I do have a physical problem" are common thoughts. The best advice is to simply acknowledge this fear as part of the old conditioning, of the brain's strategy to have you believe there is a physical problem.

A common question I hear daily is, "What should I do when I have pain, especially *a lot* of pain?" Here people acknowledge that it can be very difficult to ignore it and carry on. First, you must talk to your brain and remind yourself that you are physically fine! Tell your brain that you are on to its game, that you know about the reservoir of rage. Like Dorothy discovering the Wizard of Oz behind the curtain, you won't be fooled! The pain is not because you've done something that you are incapable of or that you are so feeble or fragile. Try to pay it as little attention as possible; the goal is for it to distract you and keep your attention and focus on pain, rather than on what may be in the unconscious. Many become obsessed with their pain—they *must* learn to shift their focus (this is the re-programming, or re-conditioning process). Try not to give in! Try to remain active, doing the activities that you enjoy.

What about medication? As medication is a physical modality, it cannot fix the problem. This fact is essential to assimilate. As I've stated earlier, use of medications can, in some circumstances, exacerbate the problem. Having said this, I do believe there are certain occasions when use of over-the-counter pain medications may be done without adding fuel to the fire. It is acceptable to take medications like acetaminophen, aspirin, ibuprofen and naproxen *if* you tell yourself, "This is **not** fixing the problem. This may take the edge off or ease some of my discomfort while I continue to do battle with my brain." Again, remember that frequent use of even these medications can worsen the situation, but used appropriately may be acceptable.

For reasons that are not entirely clear to both Dr. Sarno and myself, there is great variability in the time required for symptom resolution. This gets back to the notion of doubt. If someone states they truly believe that TMS is the problem, that they have been doing the mental homework and yet are distressed that their symptoms persist, they may question whether they have TMS. This has the elements of a catch-22. If you begin to doubt there is a psychological cause, that there *could* be a physical cause, then the work is undone and the brain's strategy of creating a physical distraction will triumph. This is part of what I refer to as *The Calendar Phenomenon*. By this time, everyone may know of someone whose symptoms vanished immediately after reading the book or shortly after seeing a physician trained in TMS treatment. So, an expectation is created in their mind that their symptoms should recede soon after incorporating this philosophy. They look at the calendar and become upset as days and weeks go by. This is where I tell people to look back at their personalities. The calendar phenomenon is another manifestation of perfectionist tendencies – it is self-imposed pressure to succeed and succeed quickly. If they can recognize this aspect of their personality and add it to their "list" of sources of stress, relief will be on the way.

Fear, doubt, the calendar phenomenon and the failure to think accurately are examples of some of the internal obstacles to healing. Several external obstacles bear mention.

#1 You have read this book and become convinced that this approach makes sense. When you mention it to your physician, he/she either dismisses it out of hand or nods indulgently, and advises a traditional regimen including medication, physical therapy, etc.

#2 You have read this book and become convinced that this approach makes sense. When you mention it to your friends, family and/or co-workers, they look at you as if you have lost your mind. They, too, may nod indulgently and then recommend a physician, practitioner, medication, herb, etc.

#3 You have read this book and become convinced that this approach makes sense. When you pick up a magazine and read an article discussing symptoms like yours, there is no mention of TMS as a possible cause. Or maybe, just maybe, there is a brief mention of

Dr. Sarno's work with TMS, but other quoted sources dismiss it out of hand. As you trust the members of the media to do their homework and provide accurate, complete information, you begin to wonder whether TMS is for real.

These scenarios occur every day. They may contribute to the conditioning that allows the pain to persist. Even in my own office, when I am introducing one of my established patients to TMS concepts, they may get angry or look at me as if I have two heads. You see, they have come in unsuspecting. They have come in to see me for evaluation of some physical symptom and did not expect to hear that it may have a psychological cause. Some are delighted, enthusiastic and quite willing to think outside of the box. To the others I explain that I can only expose them to this different way of thinking, that I cannot make them believe it. I will certainly try to make my case and be convincing, but it is ultimately up to them to decide.

Perhaps when TMS theory and treatment becomes embraced by the medical mainstream, more people will be open to this way of thinking about themselves. For those that do, it is extremely gratifying to see them succeed at getting rid of their pain and improving their quality of life. Trite as it sounds, I became a physician to help others, to help them when they are ill and keep them well. I am saddened when people refuse to accept the possibility of a psychological cause and so continue to suffer.

Chapter 31

WHAT ELSE? (Think Psychological – The Recipe)

Make a list.

Think of anything that could be a source of stress for you. Think about what makes you angry or enraged. Think of what things you worry about. Think about your personality. Identify perfectionist and/or goodist traits. Are there people in your life who did not treat you as well as you would have liked? Write all of this down. It is impossible to know what is in our unconscious (hence, the title "unconscious"), but it is possible to contemplate what might be there. By acknowledging the presence of these unpleasant thoughts and emotions, you can thwart the brain's strategy. As you undoubtedly recall, the brain's strategy is to create pain, pain that will serve as a distraction. Focusing on the pain is a type of defense mechanism – it keeps us from thinking about those things that make us upset, worried or angered. The pain keeps the reservoir of rage hidden. When we recognize that it is there and what it may contain, there is no need the pain, no further need for distraction.

Making a list is like keeping a journal. Many studies have shown that those who write regularly in a journal, about themselves, their thoughts and concerns, are healthier than those who do not journal. So, start your list or a journal, and add to it or review it regularly.

Reflect.

By now you have figured out that it is the process of self-education that will help you to feel better. It is amazing – no medication, no physical remedies and no side effects. Set aside time each day to think about TMS theory and treatment. Read and re-read this book and Dr. Sarno's books. It's not necessary to re-read everything, but it will be helpful to re-read passages that you find particularly pertinent. Even when you feel well, spend some time each day on this material. This will help you to remain well. It is good preventive medicine and I include it in my **Top 10 Lists of Things To Do To Be Healthy.**

'S TOP TEN COMMANDMENTS FOR GOOD HEALTH

1. Thou shalt exercise every day (or almost every day).

2. Thou shalt not use tobacco.

3. Thou shalt eat right.

4. Thou shalt acknowledge stress.

5. Thou shalt consume alcohol wisely.

6. Thou shalt not burn.

7. Thou shalt smile.

8. Thou shalt see thy physician.

9. Thou shalt see thy dentist, too.

10. Thou shalt take thy medication.

Discard your physical remedies.

Get rid of the special back supports, heel pads, orthotics, pillows, chair cushions, etc. They cannot fix the problem and you don't need them. Physical modalities cannot help symptoms with a psychological cause. Their very existence is part of the old conditioning and will only perpetuate the symptoms.

If you are taking narcotic pain medications, you will need to wean off of these gradually under a physician's supervision. Similarly, you should also wean off of benzodiazepines (such as Klonopin, Ativan, Valium, Xanax, etc.). These medications only mask symptoms and cannot cure them. In addition, they are physically and psychologically addicting and will only perpetuate the symptoms. They will also impair cognition and interfere with your efforts at self-education.

It is reasonable to take non-narcotic medication for pain, like aspirin, Tylenol, ibuprofen or naproxen (all available over-the-counter). However, each time you do, it is important to remind yourself that these drugs will not fix the cause of the symptoms and will just temporarily take the edge off while you continue to apply yourself mentally.

There is a myriad of other medications prescribed for the host of ailments discussed here. In most cases medication can be safely discontinued, but this should always be discussed with your physician first.

Be eternally vigilant.

Celebrate the good days. This is essential to reversing the old conditioning. Tell yourself you are indeed fine – if you had a physical problem, where did it go? However, do not be discouraged if pain returns or occurs at another location. Remember, your brain will never give up this strategy – this is how we are made. This is why it is necessary to spend some time each day reflecting. This eternal vigilance is the proverbial "ounce of prevention."

Resume activity.

You are not really well until you are back doing the activities you formerly enjoyed. While you may have to start slowly (it is still necessary to follow appropriate guidelines for exercise training), you should be able to do whatever you want. We are capable of far more than we have been told. I think very few of us approach our potential because we have been misinformed about the limits of our bodies. I have patients in their 60's, 70's and 80's running marathons, bicycling across the country, climbing mountains and participating in other strenuous activities. They are not supermen and superwomen;

they are simply folks who have taken good care of themselves and refused to believe that they are fragile.

Many people who read this and Dr. Sarno's books will be able to get better on their own, with this new knowledge. Some will not, even if they believe everything here. They may need the validation of their symptoms as TMS by a physician. There are a number of physicians in the United States who are able to diagnose and treat TMS. Several websites keep lists or links for these physicians:

www.themindbodysyndrome.com

www.premierhealthonline.com/directory.htm

http://tmshelp.com/links.htm

While I cannot speak for the other physicians treating TMS, it is clear that the diagnosis of TMS is usually suggested by the history and then supported by examination. After I take the patient's history and complete the examination, I then begin to explain TMS concepts—how very real physical symptoms may have a psychological cause. For those well versed already, this can serve to validate their symptoms and allow them to apply themselves more confidently to "thinking psychologically"—the process of self-education and thinking differently about the mind-body connection. For those new to the ideas of The Mindbody Syndrome, it gives them a new focal point, a place to start incorporating this knowledge. After the visit, I encourage all to work on this on their own, as I've outlined above, for at least several weeks. Most make gains in that time, though others do take longer (see the calendar phenomenon). I ask everyone to follow up with me via email or phone, to let me know of his or her progress. At that time I can help to clarify certain concepts or help to identify obstacles that may be interfering with improvement. Those who live near my office may return for follow up and further discussions. A not uncommon scenario is for an individual to successfully get rid of their symptoms only to experience "new" symptoms at another location. As with the initial complaint, a new history and examination often confirms that the brain has not given up its strategy and the "new" problem is again TMS. When this occurs, I have found that most are able to succeed more rapidly than they did before. This is not only gratifying but can be very empowering for my patients. It is empowering to recognize how much control we have over our bodies.

Instead of traveling to see a TMS doctor, another option would be to try and educate your own physicians. If they are open to these concepts, lend them this book or one by Dr. Sarno (or encourage them to get their own copy). They will not only then be able to help you, but should also be able to help others. By getting them to expand their knowledge base, they will be better physicians.

Chapter 32

DESPAIR AND THE LIGHT AT THE END OF THE TUNNEL

In addition to patients I have seen in my office, I have received thousands of emails and phone calls from those seeking advice, looking for relief from their pain – pain that has had dramatic effect on their lives, interfering with all manner of plans. I've had people tell me they've quit jobs, declined promotions or rejected new job offers because they felt their bodies were not up to the tasks required. In one case, a patient rejected a lucrative promotion because it meant additional time sitting in meetings and he feared this would exacerbate his symptoms. Simply sitting! He's better now. Some have put off getting married because they did not want to be a burden on their future spouse. Some have put off having children because they worried they would not be up to the physical demands of parenthood (notice I did not say the emotional demands). Others have ended their relationships and marriages because their pain was so intrusive.

Some are so desperate, suffering so much they admit they have contemplated suicide. Sadly, I know that this occurred in at least one case. This is from his wife:

Hello Dr. Sopher,

I lost my beloved husband (age 38)...this year. He committed suicide because he could not stand the RSI pain and fear for the future (losing his job, not being able to take care of his baby daughter, etc.). My husband did not suffer from any mental illness whatsoever...

My response:

I am so sorry about your husband. I am also sorry that he didn't feel he had any hope. One of the goals of my website is to provide education and inform people that there may be another explanation and treatment option for their pain. Many who suffer grow despondent and depressed.

What all of these people have in common are chronic symptoms that have failed to respond to an enormous variety of remedies.

No one should <u>ever</u> give up hope. Knowledge is indeed power and the education you receive from this book and Dr. Sarno's books should offer you hope. There is light at the end of the tunnel.

* * *

Marc D. Sopher, M.D.

BIBLIOGRAPHY

Adkins, S, Figler, R. Hip Pain in Athletes. Am Fam Phys 2000; 61: 2109-2118

Alexander, F, French, TM. Psychoanalytic Therapy. New York: the Roland Press Company, 1946

Bailer, JC. The Powerful Placebo and the Wizard of Oz. New England Journal of Medicine 2001; 344: 1630-1632

Benson, H. The Relaxation Response. New York: Avon, 1990

Benson, H. The Wellness Book. New York: Fireside, 1993.

Clark, MM. Restless Leg Syndrome. JABFP 2001; 14 (5) 368-374.

Cousins, N. Anatomy of an Illness. New York: W.W. Norton, 1979.

Craig, T, Kakumanu, S. Chronic Fatigue Syndrome: Evaluation and Treatment. American Family Physician 2002; 65: 1083-1090.

Gliatto, M. Generalized Anxiety Disorder. Am Fam Phys 2000; 62: 1591-1600

Gurshka, M, Epstein, J, Gorsky, M. Burning Mouth Syndrome. American Family Physician 2002; 65: 615-620.

Hinton, R, Moody, R, Davis, A, Thomas, S. Osteoarthritis: Diagnosis and Therapeutic Considerations. Am Fam Phys 2002; 65: 841-848.

Hrobjartsson, A, Gotzsche, P. Is the Placebo Powerless? New England Journal of Medicine 2001; 344: 1594-1602

Jensen, MC, Brant-Zawadzki, MN, Obuchowski, N., Modic, MT, Malkasian, D., Ross, JS. Magnetic Resonance Imaging of the Lumbar Spine in People Without Back Pain. New England Journal of Medicine 1994; 331:69-73

Koo, J, Lebwohl, A. Psychodermatology: The Mind and Skin Connection. Am Fam Phys 2001; 64: 1873-1878.

Larkin, M. Carpal Tunnel Syndrome Study Stirs Controversy. Lancet; Volume 357, Number 9272 16 June 2001

Longo, L, Johnson B. Addiction: Part I. Benzodiazepines – Side Effects, Abuse Risk and Alternatives. Am Fam Phys 2000; 61: 2121-2128.

McGrail, M, Lohman, W, Gorman, R. Disability Prevention Principles in the Primary Care Office. Am Fam Phys 2001; 63: 679-684.

Metts, J. Interstitial Cystitis: Urgency and Frequency Syndrome. Am Fam Phys 2001; 64:1199-1206.

Millea, P, Holloway R. Treating Fibromyalgia. Am Fam Phys 2000; 62:1575-1582

Neeck, G., Crofford, LJ. Neuroendocrine Perturbations in Fibromyalgia and Chronic Fatigue Syndrome: Rheumatic Disease Clinics of North America 2000; 26 (4)

Patel, A, Ogle, A. Diagnosis and Management of Acute Low Back Pain. Am Fam Phys 2000; 61: 1779-1786

Pert, CB. Molecules of Emotion. New York: Scribner, 1997.

Restless Legs Syndrome: Detection and Management in Primary Care. National Heart, Lung and Blood Institute Working Group on Restless Legs Syndrome. Am Fam Phys. 2000; 62: 108-114

Rosomoff, HL, Rosomoff, RS. Low Back Pain. Medical Clinics of North America 1999; 83(3): 643-663.

Sarno, JE. Healing Back Pain. New York: Warner Books, 1991.

Sarno, JE. The Mindbody Prescription. New York: Warner Books, 1998.

Siegel, BS. Love, Medicine and Miracles. New York: Harper and Row, 1986.

Siegel, BS. Peace, Love and Healing. New York: Harper and Row, 1990.

Stevens JC, Witt JC, Smith BE, Weaver AL. The frequency of carpal tunnel syndrome in computer users at a medical facility. Neurology 2001; 56:1568-1570

Swaggerty, D, Hellinger, D. Radiographic Assessment of Osteoarthritis. Am Fam Phys 2001; 64: 279-286.

Weil, A. Spontaneous Healing. New York: Knopf, 1995.

Wiesel, SW, Tsourmas, N, Feffer, HL, Citrin, CM, Patronas, N. A Study of Computer-Assisted Tomography. I. The Incidence of Positive CAT Scans in an Asymptomatic Group of Patients. Spine 1994; 9:549-51.

Woodward, T, Best, T. The Painful Shoulder: Part II. Acute and Chronic Disorders. Am Fam Phys 2000; 61: 3291-3300

Woodward, T, Best, T. The Painful Shoulder: Part I. Clinical Evaluation. Am Fam Phys 2000; 61:3079-3088

Young, C, Rutherford, D., Niedfeldt, M. Treatment of Plantar Fasciitis. Am Fam Phys 2001; 63:467-474.

Zucker, RS. Magnetic Resonance Imaging of the Lumbar Spine (letter). New England Journal of Medicine 1994; 331:1525-26.

About the Author

Dr. Marc Sopher is a family physician who has been practicing in Exeter, New Hampshire since 1990. In addition to his practice and work with TMS, he is medical director of the Synergy Health and Fitness Center and provides medical care to the students of Phillips Exeter Academy. Dr. Sopher has served on the editorial board of the American College of Sports Medicine's Health and Fitness Journal.

An avid athlete, Dr. Sopher has run seven marathons and the Mt. Washington Road Race. He was captain of the Williams College tennis team, and he continues to play competitive tennis. He enjoys biking and hiking with his family and once was spotted carrying an injured 90-pound dog on his back down Mt. Washington's Tuckerman's Ravine trail, relishing the extra workout.

CPSIA information can be obtained
at www.ICGtesting.com
Printed in the USA
BVHW082151170222
629237BV00003B/230

9 781410 707871